CHRISTIANITY OR ISLAM ~

The Contrast

Katheryn Maddox Haddad

Other Books by the Author

CHRISTIAN LIFE
Applied Christianity: Handbook 500 Good Works
You Can Be a Hero Alone
Worship Changes Since 1st Century + Worship 1sr Century Way
The Best of Alexander Campbell's Millennial Harbinger
Inside the Hearts of Bible Women-Reader+Audio+Leader
The Lord's Supper: 52 Readings with Prayers

BIBLE TEXTS
Revelation: A Love Letter From God
The Holy Spirit: 592 Verses Examined
Was Jesus God? (Why Evil)
365 Life-Changing Scriptures Day by Date
Love Letters of Jesus & His Bride, Ecclesia (Song of Solomon)
Christianity or Islam? The Contrast
The Road to Heaven

FUN BOOKS
Bible Puzzles, Bible Song Book, Bible Numbers

TOUCHING GOD SERIES
365 Golden Bible Thoughts: God's Heart to Yours
365 Pearls of Wisdom: God's Soul to Yours
365 Silver-Winged Prayers: Your Spirit to God's

SURVEY SERIES: EASY BIBLE WORKBOOKS
→Old Testament & New Testament Surveys
→Questions You Have Asked-Part I & II

HISTORICAL RESEARCH BIBLE
for Novel, Screenwriter, Documentary & Thesis Writers

HISTORICAL NOVELS & STORYBOOKS
Series of 8: They Met Jesus
Ongoing Series of 8: Intrepid Men of God
Mysteries of the Empire with Klaudius & Hektor
Christmas: They Rocked the Cradle that Rocked the World
Series of 8: A Child's Life of Christ
Series of 10: A Child's Bible Heroes
Series of 8: A Child's Bible Kids
Series of 10: A Child's Bible Ladies

GENEALOGY: Climb Your Family Tree w/o Falling Out
Volume I & 2: Beginner-Intermediate & Colonial-Medieval

Northern Lights Publishing House

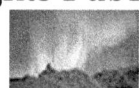

Copyright ⓒ 2014 Katheryn Maddox Haddad
ISBN-978-1-948462-62-4
Fourth Edition
Printed in the United States

TABLE OF CONTENTS

Other Books by the Author 2
Welcome 3

1. Love of Sinners 4
2. Treatment of Enemies 6
3. Attitudes of Unbelievers 11
4. Who Is Guaranteed Heaven? 12
5. Predestination of the Chosen Ones 13
6. Salvation By Works 14
7. Friendships With Unbelievers 18
8. Wife Allotments 21
9. Marriage Rights 23
10. Bowing Down 26
11. Benefits of Prophets 27
12. Punishments 31
13. Alcohol 33
14. Holy Spirit 34
15. Angels 36
16. God is One 37
17. Idolatry 38
18. End of World 39
19. Creation of Man 41
20. Fornication and Adultery 42
21. God Materializing 43
22. Heaven-Paradise 45
23. First and Last 48
24. Prayer 49
25. The Poor 50
26. Slaves or Children? 51
27. Questioning the Scriptures 55
28. Who Created Death? 56
29. How Long Sins Are Forgiven 58
30. A Few Calculations 61
31. Names 62

32. There is One God 67
33. Jesus' Life Before He Was "Born" 70
34. Prophecies of Jesus Fulfilled In His Lifetime 84
35. What Does Jesus Dying On Cross Relate to Forgiveness   94
36. Why Jesus Had to Die & Come Back To Life 101
37. Did Jesus Die? 107
38. What About Jesus' Throne Next to God? 111
39. Paul, the Anti-Christian Terrorist As Told By Paul Himself 115
40. The Bible Was Not Corrupted In the 7th Century 121
41. Proofs the Bible Was Never Corrupted 127
42. Love Letters From God to You 130
43. Gear for the Christian Soldier 136
44. Words of Courage 138
45. Some Christian Poetry 140
46. Organization of the Bible 143

47. Testimonies of 100 Muslims Who Decided Jesus Was 146
A FORMER MUSLIM'S STORY 168
48. Open Letter to Our Muslim Friends 171

Helpful Links For Further Study 181
Buy Your Next Book Now 182

About the Author 183
Connect with Katheryn Maddox Haddad 184

Get A Free Book 184
If you liked this book 184

Welcome

This book is for Christians wanting to understand Islam, and for Muslims wanting to understand Christianity. Rather than tell ABOUT what Muslims believe and what Christians believe, actual quotations are taken from the *Quran* and the *New Testament* of the *Bible (the Book)*.

It has been written with love for both Christians and Muslims.

The spellings and punctuation from the Quran have been kept the way they were translated. The spellings and punctuation from the nearly 100 Muslims who have decided Jesus really was the Son of God have been kept in the way they wrote them. These are real people.

Give a copy of this book to a friend.

1. Love of Sinners

ALLAH

Allah loveth not transgressors. [Surah 2:190]

Allah loveth not those that do wrong. [Surah 3:140]

Never will wrong-doers Find any helpers! [Surah 3:192]

Allah loves not one given to perfidy and crime. [Surah 4:107]

Those who reject Faith and do wrong, Allah will not forgive them nor guide them to any way [Surah 4:168]

Allah loves not those who do mischief. [Surah 5:64]

He loves not those who reject Faith. [Surah 30:45]

Truly Allah guides not one who transgresses and lies! Surah 40:28]

JESUS

But God demonstrates his own love for us in this: While we were still sinners, Christ died for us. [Romans 5:8]

But because of his great love for us, God, who is rich in mercy, made us alive with Christ even when we were dead in transgressions. [Ephesians 2:4-5]

God is love. We love God because he first loved us. [I John 4:8,19]

This is love: not that we loved God, but that he loved us and sent his Son as an atoning sacrifice for our sins. [I John 4:10]

2. Treatment of Enemies

ALLAH

Fight in the cause of Allah those who fight you, but do not transgress limits; for Allah loveth not transgressors. And slay them wherever ye catch them, and turn them out from where they have Turned you out; for tumult and oppression are worse than slaughter; but fight them not at the Sacred Mosque, unless they (first) fight you there; but if they fight you, slay them. Such is the reward of those who suppress faith. And fight them on until there is no more Tumult or oppression, and there prevail justice and faith in Allah. but if they cease, Let there be no hostility except to those who practice oppression. [Surah 2:190-193]

Fighting is prescribed for you, and ye dislike it. But it is possible that ye dislike a thing which is good for you, and that ye love a thing which is bad for you. But Allah knoweth, and ye know not. [Surah 2:216]

Let those fight in the cause of Allah Who sell the life of this world for the hereafter. To him who fighteth in the cause of Allah, whether he is slain or gets victory - Soon shall We give him a reward of great (value). Those who believe fight in the cause of Allah, and those who reject Faith fight in the cause of Evil: So fight ye against the friends of Satan. [Surah 4:74-75]

Then fight in Allah.s cause - Thou art held responsible only for thyself - and rouse the believers. It may be that Allah will restrain the fury of the Unbelievers; for Allah is the strongest in might and in punishment. [Surah 4:80]

But those who strive and fight Hath He distinguished above those who sit (at home) by a special reward. [Surah 4:95]

"I will instill terror into the hearts of the Unbelievers: smite ye above their necks and smite all their finger-tips off them." [Surah 8:12]

And fight with them on until there is no more persecution or oppression, and religion becomes Allah's in its entirety. [Surah 8:39]

Against them make ready your strength to the utmost of your power, including steeds of war, to strike terror into (the hearts of) the enemies, of Allah and your enemies. [Surah 8:59]

O Messenger. rouse the Believers to the fight. [Surah 8:65]

Those who believe, and emigrate to fight for the Faith, in the cause of Allah as well as those who give (them) asylum and aid, these are (all) in very truth the Believers: for them is the forgiveness of sins and a provision most generous. [Surah 8:74]

But when the forbidden months are past, then fight and slay the Pagans wherever ye find them, and seize them, beleaguer them, and lie in wait for them in every stratagem (of war). [Surah 9:5]

Fight them, and Allah will punish them by your hands, cover them with shame, help you (to victory) over them. [Surah 9:14]

Fight those who believe not in Allah nor the Last Day, nor hold that forbidden which hath been forbidden by Allah and His Messenger, nor acknowledge the religion of Truth, (even if they are) of the People of the Book [Jews & Christians]. [Surah 9:29]

O ye who believe! fight the unbelievers who gird you about, and let them find firmness in you: and know that Allah is with those who fear Him. [Surah 9:123]

Therefore, when ye meet the Unbelievers (in fight), smite at their necks. [Surah 47:44]

Say to the desert Arabs who lagged behind: "Ye shall be summoned (to fight) against a people given to vehement war: then shall ye fight, or they shall submit. Then if ye show obedience, Allah will grant you a goodly reward, but if ye turn back as ye did before, He will punish you with a grievous Penalty." [Surah 48:16]

Truly Allah loves those who fight in His Cause in battle array, as if they were a solid cemented structure. [Surah 61:4]

JESUS

39But I tell you, do not resist an evil person. If someone strikes you on the right cheek, turn to him the other also. 40And if someone wants to sue you and take your tunic, let him have your cloak as well. 41If someone forces you to go one mile, go with him two miles. 42Give to the one who asks you, and do not turn away from the one who wants to borrow from you.
43"You have heard that it was said, 'Love your neighbor and hate your enemy.' 44But I tell you: Love your enemies and pray for those who persecute you, 45that you may be sons of your Father in heaven. He causes his sun to rise on the evil and the good, and sends rain on the righteous and the unrighteous. 46If you love those who love you, what reward will you get? Are not even the tax collectors doing that? 47And if you greet only your brothers, what are you doing more than others? Do not even pagans do that? [Matthew 5:39-47]

27"But I tell you who hear me: Love your enemies, do good to those who hate you, 28bless those who curse you, pray for those who mistreat you. 29If someone strikes you on one cheek, turn to him the other also. If someone takes your cloak, do not stop him from taking your tunic. 30Give to everyone who asks you, and if anyone takes what belongs to you, do not demand it back. 31Do to others as you would have them do to you.

32"If you love those who love you, what credit is that to you? Even 'sinners' love those who love them. 33And if you do good to those who are good to you, what credit is that to you? Even 'sinners' do that. 34And if you lend to those from whom you expect repayment, what credit is that to you? Even 'sinners' lend to 'sinners,' expecting to be repaid in full. 35But love your enemies, do good to them, and lend to them without expecting to get anything back. Then your reward will be great, and you will be sons of the Most High, because he is kind to the ungrateful and wicked. 36Be merciful, just as your Father is merciful. [Luke 6:27-36]

There they crucified him, along with the criminals — one on his right, the other on his left. Jesus said, "Father, forgive them, for they do not know what they are doing." [Luke 23:33-34]

While they were stoning him, Stephen prayed, "Lord Jesus, receive my spirit." 60Then he fell on his knees and cried out, "Lord, do not hold this sin against them." [Acts 7:59-60]

If it is possible, as far as it depends on you, live at peace with everyone. [Romans 12:18]

If your enemy is hungry, feed him; if he is thirsty, give him something to drink. [Romans 12:20]

Do not be overcome by evil, but overcome evil with good. [Romans 12:21]

When we are cursed, we bless; when we are persecuted, we endure it; 13when we are slandered, we answer kindly. [I Corinthians 4:12-13]

When they hurled their insults at him, he did not retaliate; when he suffered, he made no threats. [I Peter 2:23]

Do not repay evil with evil or insult with insult, but with blessing, because to this you were called so that you may inherit a blessing. [I Peter 3:9]

3. Attitudes of Unbelievers

ALLAH

Unbelievers May attack you: For the Unbelievers are unto you open enemies. Unbelievers wish, if ye were negligent of your arms and your baggage, to assault you in a single rush. [Surah 4:101-102]

It is never the wish of those without Faith among the People of the Book, nor of the Pagans, that anything good should come down to you from your Lord. [Surah 2:105]

JESUS

But I tell you who hear me: Love your enemies, do good to those who hate you, 28bless those who curse you, pray for those who mistreat you. [Matthew 5:27]

4. Who Is Guaranteed Heaven?

ALLAH

Those who leave their homes in the cause of Allah, and are then slain or die, On them will Allah bestow verily a goodly Provision: Truly Allah is He Who bestows the best provision. [Surah 22:58]

But those who are slain in the Way of Allah, He will never let their deeds be lost. [Surah 47:4]

JESUS

For it is by grace you have been saved, through faith—and this not from yourselves, it is the gift of God— 9not by works, so that no one can boast. [Ephesians 2:8]

5. Predestination of the Chosen Ones

ALLAH

5-But Allah will choose for His special Mercy whom He will [Surah 2:104]

He guides whom He wills to the Straight way." [Surah 2:142]

He forgiveth whom He pleaseth, and He punisheth whom He pleaseth. [Surah 5:18]

He punishes whom He pleases, and He grants Mercy to whom He pleases. [Surah 29:21]

For Allah leaves to stray whom He wills, and guides whom He wills. So let not thy soul go out in (vainly) sighing after them: for Allah knows well all that they do. [Surah 35:8]

JESUS

This is good, and pleases God our Savior, who wants all men to be saved and to come to a knowledge of the truth. [I Timothy 2:3-4]

For the grace of God that brings salvation has appeared to all men. [Titus 2:11]

The Lord…is not wanting anyone to perish, but everyone to come to repentance. [II Peter 3:9]

6. Salvation By Works

ALLAH

For them there will be allotted a share for what they have earned. And Allah is Swift at reckoning. [Surah 2:202]

And be afraid of the Day when you shall be brought back to Allah. Then every person shall be paid what he earned, and they shall not be dealt with unjustly. [Surah 2:281]

But those who believe and do deeds of righteousness, We shall soon admit to Gardens. But those who believe and do deeds of righteousness, we shall soon admit them to gardens. If any do deeds of righteousness, be they male or female - and have faith, they will enter Heaven. [Surah 4:57, 122, 124]

We shall set up scales of justice for the Day of Judgment, so that not a soul will be dealt with unjustly in the least, and if there be (no more than) the weight of a mustard seed, We will bring it (to account): and enough are We to take account. [Surah 21:47]

Verily Allah will admit those who believe and work righteous deeds, to Gardens. Allah will admit those who believe and work righteous deeds [Surah 22:14,23]

Those who believe and work righteous deeds, from them shall We blot out all evil (that may be) in them, and We shall reward them according to the best of their deeds. [Surah 29:7]

That He may reward those who believe and work righteous deeds, out of his Bounty. [Surah 30:45]

If any one does a righteous deed, it ensures to the benefit of his own soul; if he does evil, it works against (his own soul).

[Surah 45:15]

And to all are (assigned) degrees according to the deeds which they (have done), and in order that (Allah) may recompense their deeds, and no injustice be done to them. [Surah 46:19]

Behold, two (guardian angels) appointed to learn (his doings) learn (and noted them), one sitting on the right and one on the left. Not a word does he utter but there is a sentinel by him, ready (to note it). [Surah 50:17-18]

Those who avoid great sins and indecent deeds, only (falling into) small faults – certainly, your Lord is ample in forgiveness.

We sent aforetime our apostles with Clear Signs and sent down with them the Book and the Balance (of Right and Wrong), that men may stand forth in justice. [Surah 57:25]

Then shall anyone who has done an atom's weight of good, see it! And anyone who has done an atom's weight of evil, shall see it. [Surah 99:7-8]

Then he whose balance (of good deeds) will be (found) heavy, will be in a Life of good pleasure and satisfaction. But he whose balance (of good deeds) will be (found) light – Will have his home in a (bottomless) Pit. And what will explain to you what this is? (It is) a Fire blazing fiercely! [Surah 101:6-10]

JESUS

For all have sinned and fall short of the glory of God, and are justified freely by his grace through the redemption that came by Christ Jesus. God presented him as a sacrifice of atonement, through faith in his blood. He did this to demonstrate his justice, because in his forbearance he had left the sins committed beforehand unpunished. Where, then, is the boasting? [Romans 3:23-25, 27]

If, in fact, Abraham was justified by works, he had something to boast about—but not before God. What does the Scripture say? "Abraham believed God, and it was credited to him as righteousness." [Romans 4:2-3]

But God demonstrates his own love for us in this: While we were still sinners, Christ died for us. [Romans 5:8]

What shall we say, then? Shall we go on sinning so that grace may increase? 2By no means! We died to sin; how can we live in it any longer? 3Or don't you know that all of us who were baptized into Christ Jesus were baptized into his death? 4We were therefore buried with him through baptism into death in order that, just as Christ was raised from the dead through the glory of the Father, we too may live a new life.

5If we have been united with him like this in his death, we will certainly also be united with him in his resurrection. 6For we know that our old self was crucified with him so that the body of sin might be done away with, that we should no longer be slaves to sin— 7because anyone who has died has been freed from sin. [Romans 6:1-7]

He who did not spare his own Son, but gave him up for us all—how will he not also, along with him, graciously give us all things? [Romans 8:32]

No, in all these things we are more than conquerors through him who loved us. For I am convinced that neither death nor life, neither angels nor demons, neither the present nor the future, nor any powers, neither height nor depth, nor anything else in all creation, will be able to separate us from the love of God that is in Christ Jesus our Lord. [Romans 8:37-39]

Therefore, I urge you, brothers, in view of God's mercy, to offer your bodies as living sacrifices, holy and pleasing to God — this is your spiritual act of worship. [Romans 12:1]

But because of his great love for us, God, who is rich in mercy, 5made us alive with Christ even when we were dead in transgressions — it is by grace you have been saved. [Ephesians 2:5]

For it is by grace you have been saved, through faith — and this not from yourselves, it is the gift of God — not by works, so that no one can boast. [Ephesians 2:8-9]

…,by the power of God, who has saved us and called us to a holy life — not because of anything we have done but because of his own purpose and grace. This grace was given us in Christ Jesus before the beginning of time, but it has now been revealed through the appearing of our Savior, Christ Jesus, who has destroyed death. [II Timothy 1:8-10]

But when the kindness and love of God our Savior appeared, 5he saved us, not because of righteous things we had done, but because of his mercy. He saved us through the washing of rebirth and renewal by the Holy Spirit, 6whom he poured out on us generously through Jesus Christ our Savior, 7so that, having been justified by his grace, we might become heirs having the hope of eternal life. [Titus 3:4-7]

7. Friendships With Unbelievers

ALLAH

Let not the believers Take for friends or helpers Unbelievers rather than believers: if any do that, in nothing will there be help from Allah. [Surah 3:28]

O ye who believe! Take not into your intimacy those outside your ranks: They will not fail to corrupt you. They only desire your ruin: Rank hatred has already appeared from their mouths: What their hearts conceal is far worse. We have made plain to you the Signs, if ye have wisdom. [Surah 3:118]

If aught that is good befalls you, it grieves them; but if some misfortune overtakes you, they rejoice at it. But if ye are constant and do right, not the least harm will their cunning do to you; for Allah Compasseth round about all that they do. [Surah 3:20]

But take not friends from their ranks until they flee in the way of Allah (From what is forbidden). But if they turn renegades, seize them and slay them wherever ye find them; and (in any case) take no friends or helpers from their ranks. [Surah 4:89]

Yea, to those who take for friends unbelievers rather than believers: is it honour they seek among them? Nay. [Surah 4:139]

Take not for friends unbelievers rather than believers: Do ye wish to offer Allah an open proof against yourselves? [Surah 4:144]

O ye who believe! take not the Jews and the Christians for your friends and protectors: They are but friends and protectors to each other. [Surah 5:51]

Take not my enemies and yours as friends (or protectors), offering them (your) love, even though they have rejected the Truth that has come to you, and have (on the contrary) driven out the Prophet and yourselves (from your homes), (simply) because ye believe in Allah your Lord! If ye have come out to strive in My Way and to seek My Good Pleasure, (take them not as friends), holding secret converse of love (and friendship) with them: for I know full well all that ye conceal and all that ye reveal. And any of you that does this has strayed from the Straight Path. [Surah 60:1]

Turn not (for friendship) to people on whom is the Wrath of Allah, of the Hereafter they are already in despair, just as the Unbelievers are in despair about those (buried) in graves. Surah 60:13]

JESUS

The Son of Man came eating and drinking, and they say, 'Here is a glutton and a drunkard, a friend of tax collectors and "sinners." ' But wisdom is proved right by her actions." [Matthew 11:19]

Come to me, all you who are weary and burdened, and I will give you rest. 29Take my yoke upon you and learn from me, for I am gentle and humble in heart, and you will find rest for your souls. 30For my yoke is easy and my burden is light." [Matthew 11:28-30]

The Son of Man came eating and drinking, and you say, 'Here is a glutton and a drunkard, a friend of tax collectors and "sinners." ' [Luke 7:34]

When a woman who had lived a sinful life in that town learned that Jesus was eating at the Pharisee's house, she brought an alabaster jar of perfume, 38and as she stood behind him at his feet weeping, she began to wet his feet with her tears. Then she wiped them with her hair, kissed them and poured perfume on them.

39When the Pharisee who had invited him saw this, he said to himself, "If this man were a prophet, he would know who is touching him and what kind of woman she is—that she is a sinner." [Luke 7:37-39]

For the Son of Man came to seek and to save what was lost." [Luke 19:10]

To the weak I became weak, to win the weak. I have become all things to all men so that by all possible means I might save some. [I Corinthians 9:22]

Here is a trustworthy saying that deserves full acceptance: Christ Jesus came into the world to save sinners—of whom I am the worst. 16But for that very reason I was shown mercy so that in me, the worst of sinners, Christ Jesus might display his unlimited patience as an example for those who would believe on him and receive eternal life. [I Timothy 1:15-16]

8. Wife Allotments

ALLAH

Marry women of your choice, Two or three or four; but if ye fear that ye shall not be able to deal justly (with them), then only one, or (a captive) that your right hands possess, that will be more suitable, to prevent you from doing injustice. [Surah 4:3]

If any of you have not the means wherewith to wed free believing women, they may wed believing girls. [Surah 4:25]

O Prophet! We have made lawful to thee thy wives to whom thou hast paid their dowers; and those whom thy right hand possesses out of the prisoners of war whom Allah has assigned to thee; and daughters of thy paternal uncles and aunts, and daughters of thy maternal uncles and aunts, who migrated (from Makka) with thee; and any believing woman who dedicates her soul to the Prophet if the Prophet wishes to wed her; this only for thee [Mohammed], and not for the Believers (at large). [Surah 33:50]

And those who guard their chastity, except with their wives and the (captives) whom their right hands possess – for (then) they are not to be blamed. [Surah 70:29-30]

JESUS

Now the overseer must be above reproach, the husband of but one wife, temperate, self-controlled, respectable, hospitable, able to teach, 3not given to drunkenness, not violent but gentle, not quarrelsome, not a lover of money. 4He must manage his own family well and see that his children obey him with proper respect. [I Timothy 3:2-4]

An elder must be blameless, the husband of but one wife, a man whose children believe and are not open to the charge of being wild and disobedient. 7Since an overseer[b] is entrusted with God's work, he must be blameless—not overbearing, not quick-tempered, not given to drunkenness, not violent, not pursuing dishonest gain. 8Rather he must be hospitable, one who loves what is good, who is self-controlled, upright, holy and disciplined. [Titus 1:6-8]

Now as the church submits to Christ, so also wives should submit to their husbands in everything. Husbands, love your wives, just as Christ loved the church and gave himself up for her 26to make her holy, cleansing her by the washing with water through the word, 27and to present her to himself as a radiant church, without stain or wrinkle or any other blemish, but holy and blameless. 28In this same way, husbands ought to love their wives as their own bodies. He who loves his wife loves himself. 29After all, no one ever hated his own body, but he feeds and cares for it, just as Christ does the church. [Ephesians 5:24-29]

9. Marriage Rights

ALLAH

Allah (thus) directs you as regards your Children's (inheritance): to the male, a portion equal to that of two females. [Surah 4:11]

About those who leave no descendants or ascendants as heirs....the male having twice the share of the female. [Surah 4:176]

Also (prohibited are) women already married, except those whom your right hands possess. And those who guard their chastity, except with their wives and the (captives) whom their right hands possess [Surah 4:24; 70:29-30]

It is not lawful for thee (to marry more) women after this....except any thy right hand should possess (as handmaidens): and Allah doth watch over all things. [Surah 33:52]

O ye who believe! When there come to you believing women refugees, examine (and test) them....They are not lawful (wives) for the Unbelievers, nor are the (Unbelievers) lawful (husbands) for them. But pay the Unbelievers what they have spent (on their dower), and there will be no blame on you if ye marry them on payment of their dower to them. [Surah 60:10)

If any of you have not the means wherewith to wed free believing women, they may wed believing girls from among those whom your right hands possess. [Surah 4:25].

When ye do divorce women, divorce them at their prescribed periods, and count (accurately), their prescribed periods.... Such of your women as have passed the age of monthly courses, for them the prescribed period, if ye have any doubts, is three months, and for those who have no courses (yet). [Surah 65:1, 4]

And say to the believing women that they should lower their gaze and guard their modesty; that they should not display their beauty and ornaments except what (must ordinarily) appear thereof; that they should draw their veils over their bosoms and not display their beauty except to their [family members]. [Surah 24:31]

JESUS

There is neither Jew nor Greek, slave nor free, male nor female, for you are all one in Christ Jesus. [Galatians 3:28]

"It has been said, 'But I tell you that anyone who divorces his wife, except for sexual immorality, makes her the victim of adultery, and anyone who marries a divorced woman commits adultery. [Matthew 5:31-32]

For example, by law a married woman is bound to her husband as long as he is alive, but if her husband dies, she is released from the law that binds her to him. [Romans 7:2]

To the married I give this command (not I, but the Lord): A wife must not separate from her husband. 11 But if she does, she must remain unmarried or else be reconciled to her husband. And a husband must not divorce his wife.

12 To the rest I say this (I, not the Lord): If any brother has a wife who is not a believer and she is willing to live with him, he must not divorce her. 13 And if a woman has a husband who is not a believer and he is willing to live with her, she must not divorce him. 14 For the unbelieving husband has been sanctified

through his wife, and the unbelieving wife has been sanctified through her believing husband. Otherwise your children would be unclean, but as it is, they are holy.

16 How do you know, wife, whether you will save your husband? Or, how do you know, husband, whether you will save your wife? [I Corinthians 7:10-16]

I also want the women to dress modestly, with decency and propriety, adorning themselves, not with elaborate hairstyles or gold or pearls or expensive clothes, 10 but with good deeds, appropriate for women who profess to worship God. [I Timothy 2:9-10]

Your beauty should not come from outward adornment, such as elaborate hairstyles and the wearing of gold jewelry or fine clothes. 4 Rather, it should be that of your inner self, the unfading beauty of a gentle and quiet spirit, which is of great worth in God's sight. I Peter 3:9-10]

10. Bowing Down

ALLAH

And (remember) when We said to the angels: "Prostrate yourselves before Adam." And they prostrated. [Surah 2:34]

"When I have fashioned him (in due proportion) and breathed into him of My spirit, fall ye down in obeisance unto him [Adam]." So the angels prostrated themselves, all of them together. [Surah 15:29-30]

JESUS

As Peter entered the house, Cornelius met him and fell at his feet in reverence. But Peter made him get up. "Stand up," he said, "I am only a man myself." [Acts 10:25-26]

At this I fell at his [angel's] feet to worship him. But he said to me, "Do not do it! I am a fellow servant with you and with your brothers who hold to the testimony of Jesus. Worship God!" [Revelation 19:10]

11. Benefits of Prophets

ALLAH

...disobey the apostle will wish that the earth Were made one with them: But never will they hide a single fact from Allah. [Surah 4:41]

We sent not an apostle, but to be obeyed, in accordance with the will of Allah. [Surah 4:64]

He who obeys the Messenger, obeys Allah. But if any turn away, We have not sent thee to watch over their (evil deeds). [Surah 4:80]

If anyone contends with the Messenger...and follows a path other than becoming to men of Faith, We shall...land him in Hell. [Surah 4:115]

The punishment of those who wage war against Allah and His Messenger, and strive with might and main for mischief through the land is: execution, or crucifixion, or the cutting off of hands and feet from opposite sides, or exile from the land: that is their disgrace in this world, and a heavy punishment is theirs in the Hereafter. [Surah 5:33]

But those who molest the Messenger will have a grievous penalty. Know they not that for those who oppose Allah and His Messenger, is the Fire of Hell?- [Surah 9:61,63]

It was not fitting for the people of Medina and the Bedouin Arabs of the neighbourhood, to refuse to follow Allah's Messenger, nor to prefer their own lives to his. [Surah 9:120]

Deem not the summons of the Messenger among yourselves like the summons of one of you to another: Allah doth know those of you who slip away under shelter of some excuse: then let those beware who withstand the Messenger's order, lest some trial befall them, or a grievous penalty be inflicted on them. [Surah 24:63]

O consorts of the Prophet! If any of you were guilty of evident unseemly conduct, the Punishment would be doubled to her, and that is easy for Allah. [Surah 33:30]

Then when Zaid had dissolved (his marriage) with her, with the necessary (formality), We joined her in marriage to thee: in order that (in future) there may be no difficulty to the Believers in (the matter of) marriage with the wives of their adopted sons, when the latter have dissolved with the necessary (formality) (their marriage) with them. And Allah's command must be fulfilled. [Surah 33:37]

O ye who believe! Enter not the Prophet's houses, until leave is given you, for a meal, (and then) not (so early as) to wait for its preparation: but when ye are invited, enter; and when ye have taken your meal, disperse, without seeking familiar talk. Such (behaviour) annoys the Prophet. [Surah 33:53]

Those who annoy Allah and His Messenger - Allah has cursed them in this World and in the Hereafter, and has prepared for them a humiliating Punishment. [Surah 33:7]

O ye who believe! Raise not your voices above the voice of the Prophet, nor speak aloud to him in talk, as ye may speak aloud to one another, lest your deeds become vain and ye perceive not. Those that lower their voices in the presence of Allah's Messenger – their hearts has Allah tested for piety: For them is Forgiveness and a great Reward. [Surah 49:2-3]

PROPHETS OF JESUS

ELIJAH: Then the word of the Lord came to Elijah: "Leave here, turn eastward and hide in the Kerith Ravine, east of the Jordan." Elijah was afraid and ran for his life....I "I am the only one left, and now they are trying to kill me too." He is a man with a garment of hair and with a leather belt around his waist. [I Kings 17:2-3; 19:3,10; II Kings 1:8]

ISAIAH: Then the LORD said, "Just as my servant Isaiah has gone stripped and barefoot for three years...." [Isaiah 20:3]

JEREMIAH: "Ah, Sovereign LORD," I [Jeremiah] said, "I do not know how to speak; I am only a child." 7 But the LORD said to me, "Do not say, 'I am only a child.' You must go to everyone I send you to and say whatever I command you. 8 Do not be afraid of them, for I am with you and will rescue you," declares the LORD. [Jeremiah 1:6-8]

EZEKIEL: As he spoke, the Spirit came into me and raised me to my feet, and I heard him speaking to me. 3 He said: "Son of man, I am sending you to the Israelites, to a rebellious nation that has rebelled against me.... And you, son of man, do not be afraid of them or their words. Do not be afraid, though briers and thorns are all around you and you live among scorpions. Do not be afraid of what they say or terrified by them, though they are a rebellious house. 7 You must speak my words to them, whether they listen or fail to listen. [Ezekiel 2:1-7]

JOHN THE BAPTIST: His father Zechariah was filled with the Holy Spirit and prophesied: And you, my child [John the Baptist], will be called a prophet of the Most High; for you will go on before the Lord to prepare the way for him.... [When grown] John's clothes were made of camel's hair, and he had a leather belt around his waist. His food was locusts and wild honey. 5People went out to him from Jerusalem and all Judea and the whole region of the Jordan. 6Confessing their sins, they were baptized by him in the Jordan River. [Luke 1:67, 76; Matthew 3:4-6]

12. Punishments

ALLAH

As to the thief, Male or female, cut off his or her hands: a punishment by way of example, from Allah, for their crime: and Allah is Exalted in power. [Surah 5:38]

The punishment of those who wage war against Allah and His Messenger, and strive with might and main for mischief through the land is: execution, or crucifixion, or the cutting off of hands and feet from opposite sides. [Surah 5:33]

"Be sure I will cut off your hands and your feet on apposite sides, and I will cause you all to die on the cross." [Surah 7:124]

We ordained therein for them: "Life for life, eye for eye, nose or nose, ear for ear, tooth for tooth, and wounds equal for equal." [Surah 5:45]

I will instil terror into the hearts of the Unbelievers: smite ye above their necks and smite all their finger-tips off them." This because they contended against Allah and His Messenger. If any contend against Allah and His Messenger, Allah is strict in punishment. [Surah 8:12-13]

Therefore, when ye meet the Unbelievers (in fight), smite at their necks. [Surah 47:4]

Those who incurred the curse of Allah and His wrath, those of whom some He transformed into apes and swine, those who worshipped evil. [Surah 5:60]

JESUS

You have heard that it was said, 'Eye for eye, and tooth for tooth.' 39BUT I tell you, Do not resist an evil person. If someone strikes you on the right cheek, turn to him the other also. 40And if someone wants to sue you and take your tunic, let him have your cloak as well. 41If someone forces you to go one mile, go with him two miles. 42Give to the one who asks you, and do not turn away from the one who wants to borrow from you. [Matthew 5:38-42]

Brothers and sisters, if someone is caught in a sin, you who live by the Spirit should restore that person gently. But watch yourselves, or you also may be tempted. [Galatians 6:1]

Anyone who has been stealing must steal no longer, but must work, doing something useful with their own hands, that they may have something to share with those in need. [Ephesians 4:28]

Do not repay evil with evil or insult with insult. On the contrary, repay evil with blessing, because to this you were called so that you may inherit a blessing. [I Peter 3:9]

Do not repay anyone evil for evil. Be careful to do what is right in the eyes of everyone. 18 If it is possible, as far as it depends on you, live at peace with everyone. [Romans 12:17-18]

13. Alcohol

ALLAH

O ye who believe! Intoxicants and gambling, (dedication of) stones, and (divination by) arrows, are an abomination, of Satan's handwork: eschew such (abomination), that ye may prosper. [Surah 5:90]

CHRIST

Do not get drunk on wine, which leads to debauchery. Instead, be filled with the Spirit. 19Speak to one another with psalms, hymns and spiritual songs. Sing and make music in your heart to the Lord, 20always giving thanks to God the Father for everything, in the name of our Lord Jesus Christ. 21Submit to one another out of reverence for Christ. [Ephesians 5:18-21]

14. Holy Spirit

ALLAH

We gave Moses the Book and followed him up with a succession of apostles; We gave Jesus the son of Mary Clear (Signs) and strengthened him with the Holy Spirit. [Surah 2:87]

Christ Jesus the son of Mary was an apostle of Allah, and His Word, which He bestowed on Mary, and a Spirit proceeding from Him. [Surah 4:171]

Then will Allah say: "O Jesus the son of Mary! Recount My favour to thee and to thy mother. Behold! I strengthened thee with the Holy Spirit. [Surah 5:110]

Say, the Holy Spirit has brought the revelation from thy Lord in Truth. [Surah 16:102]

And (remember) her who guarded her chastity: We breathed into her of Our Spirit, and We made her and her son a sign for all peoples. [Surah 21:91]

And Mary the daughter of 'Imran, who guarded her chastity; and We breathed into (her body) of Our Spirit; and she testified to the truth of the words of her Lord and of His Revelations, and was one of the devout (servants). [Surah 66:12]

The angels and the Spirit ascend unto him in a Day the measure whereof is (as) fifty thousand years: [Surah 70:4]

The Day that the Spirit and the angels will stand forth in ranks, none shall speak except any who is permitted by (Allah) Most Gracious, and He will say what is right. [Surah 78:38]

JESUS

But after he had considered this, an angel of the Lord appeared to him in a dream and said, "Joseph son of David, do not be afraid to take Mary home as your wife, because what is conceived in her is from the Holy Spirit. 21She will give birth to a son, and you are to give him the name Jesus,[c] because he will save his people from their sins." [Matthew 1:20-21]

On the evening of that first day of the week, when the disciples [12 apostles] were together, with the doors locked for fear of the Jews, Jesus came and stood among them [after coming back to life] and said, "Peace be with you!" 20After he said this, he showed them his hands and side [from the crucifixion]. The disciples were overjoyed when they saw the Lord. 21Again Jesus said, "Peace be with you! As the Father has sent me, I am sending you." 22And with that he breathed on them and said, "Receive the Holy Spirit. [John 20:19-21]

"Therefore let all Israel be assured of this: God has made this Jesus, whom you crucified, both Lord and Christ." 37When the people heard this, they were cut to the heart and said to Peter and the other apostles, "Brothers, what shall we do?" 38Peter replied, "Repent and be baptized, every one of you, in the name of Jesus Christ for the forgiveness of your sins. And you will receive the gift of the Holy Spirit. 39The promise is for you and your children and for all who are far off. [Acts 2:36-39]

Make every effort to keep the unity of the Spirit through the bond of peace. 4There is one body and one Spirit—just as you were called to one hope when you were called— 5one Lord, one faith, one baptism; 6one God and Father of all, who is over all and through all and in all. [Ephesians 4:3-6]

15. Angels

ALLAH

At length, when death approaches one of you, Our angels take his soul, and they never fail in their duty. [Surah 6:61]

For each (such person) there are (angels) in succession, before and behind him: They guard him by command of Allah. [Surah 13:11]

But verily over you (are appointed angels) to protect you – Kind and honourable – writing down (your deeds). [Surah 81:11-12]

JESUS

[Jesus said] "See that you do not look down on one of these little ones [children]. For I tell you that their angels in heaven always see the face of my Father in heaven." [Matthew 18:10]

The time came when the beggar died and the angels carried him to Abraham's side. [Luke 16:22]

Are not all angels ministering spirits sent to serve those who will inherit salvation? [Hebrews 1:14]

16. God is One

ALLAH

Christ Jesus the son of Mary was an apostle of Allah, and His Word, which He bestowed on Mary, and a Spirit proceeding from Him. [Surah 4:171]

Had it not been for a Word that went forth before from thy Lord, (their punishment) must necessarily have come; but there is a Term appointed (for respite). [Surah 20:129]

They do blaspheme who say: Allah is one of three in a Trinity: for there is no god except One Allah. If they desist not from their word (of blasphemy), verily a grievous penalty will befall the blasphemers among them. [Surah 5:73]

JESUS

In the beginning was the Word, and the Word was with God, and the Word was God. 2He was with God in the beginning. 3Through him all things were made; without him nothing was made that has been made. The Word became flesh and made his dwelling among us. We have seen his glory, the glory of the One and Only, who came from the Father, full of grace and truth. The next day John saw Jesus coming toward him and said, "Look, the Lamb of God, who takes away the sin of the world!" [John 1:1-3, 14, 29]

For there are three that bear witness in heaven: the Father, the Word, and the Holy Spirit; and these three are one. [I John 5:7]

17. Idolatry

ALLAH

18-Seest thou not that to Allah bow down in worship all things that are in the heavens and on earth, the sun, the moon, the stars; the hills, the trees, the animals; and a great number among mankind. [Surah 22:18]

He said: "worship ye that which ye have (yourselves) carved? [Surah 37:95]

JESUS

While [the apostle] Paul was waiting for them in Athens, he was greatly distressed to see that the city was full of idols Paul then stood up in the meeting of the Areopagus and said: "Men of Athens! I see that in every way you are very religious. 23For as I walked around and looked carefully at your objects of worship, I even found an altar with this inscription: TO AN UNKNOWN GOD. Now what you worship as something unknown I am going to proclaim to you. 24"The God who made the world and everything in it is the Lord of heaven and earth and does not live in temples built by hands. 25And he is not served by human hands, as if he needed anything, because he himself gives all men life and breath and everything else. 26From one man he made every nation of men. [Acts 17:16, 22-26]

18. End of World

ALLAH

The Day that We roll up the heavens like a scroll rolled up for books (completed). [Surah 21:104]

And the Day that the trumpet will be sounded - then will be smitten with terror those who are in the heavens, and those who are on earth, except such as Allah will please (to exempt): and all shall come to His (Presence) as beings conscious of their lowliness. [Surah 27:87]

Then, when one blast is sounded on the trumpet, And the earth is moved, and its mountains, and they are crushed to powder at one stroke – On that Day shall the (Great) Event come to pass. And the sky will be rent asunder. [Surah 69:13-16]

And thy Lord cometh, and His angels, rank upon rank, [Surah 89:22]

JESUS

There was a great earthquake. The sun turned black like sackcloth made of goat hair, the whole moon turned blood red, 13and the stars in the sky fell to earth, as late figs drop from a fig tree when shaken by a strong wind. 14The sky receded like a scroll, rolling up, and every mountain and island was removed from its place. [Revelation 6:12-14]

I declare to you, brothers, that flesh and blood cannot inherit the kingdom of God, nor does the perishable inherit the imperishable. 51Listen, I tell you a mystery: We will not all sleep, but we will all be changed— 52in a flash, in the twinkling of an eye, at the last trumpet. For the trumpet will sound, the dead will be raised imperishable, and we will be changed. [I Corinthians 15:50-52]

"At that time the sign of the Son of Man will appear in the sky, and all the nations of the earth will mourn. They will see the Son of Man coming on the clouds of the sky, with power and great glory. 31And he will send his angels with a loud trumpet call, and they will gather his elect from the four winds, from one end of the heavens to the other. [Matthew 24:30-31]

19. Creation of Man

ALLAH

Man We did create from a quintessence (of clay). [Surah 23:12]

JESUS

The LORD God formed the man from the dust of the ground and breathed into his nostrils the breath of life, and the man became a living being. [Genesis 2:7]

20. Fornication and Adultery

ALLAH

The fornicatress and the fornicator, flog each of them with a hundred stripes. Let not pity withhold you in their case, in a punishment prescribed by Allah, if you believe in Allah and the Last Day. And let a party of the believers witness their punishment. (This punishment is for unmarried persons guilty of the above crime, but if married persons commit it (illegal sex), the punishment is to stone them to death, according to Allah's Law). [Surah 24:2, MKV]

Would ye really approach men in your lusts rather than women? Nay, ye are a people (grossly) ignorant! [Surah 27:55]

JESUS

The teachers of the law and the Pharisees brought in a woman caught in adultery. They made her stand before the group 4and said to Jesus, "Teacher, this woman was caught in the act of adultery. 5In the Law Moses commanded us to stone such women. Now what do you say?"

"If any one of you is without sin, let him be the first to throw a stone at her." Jesus straightened up and asked her, "Woman, where are they? Has no one condemned you?" 11"No one, sir," she said. "Then neither do I condemn you," Jesus declared. "Go now and leave your life of sin." [John 8:3-5, 7, 10-11]

21. God Materializing

ALLAH

But when he came to the (fire), a voice was heard from the right bank of the valley, from a tree in hallowed ground: "O Moses! Verily I am Allah, the Lord of the Worlds.... [Surah 28:30]

He was taught by one Mighty in Power, Endued with Wisdom: For he appeared (in stately form) while he was in the highest part of the horizon: Then he approached and came closer, and was at a distance of but two bow-lengths or (even) nearer. So did (Allah) convey the inspiration to His Servant – (conveyed) what He (meant) to convey. The (Prophet's) (mind and) heart in no way falsified that which he saw. Will you then dispute with him concerning what he saw? For indeed he saw him at a second descent. (His) sight never swerved, nor did it go wrong! For truly did he see, of the Signs of his Lord, the Greatest! [Surah 55:5-13, 17-18]

Surely, this is the word of a most honourable Messenger, Endued with Power, held in honour by the Lord of the throne, With authority there (and) faithful to his trust. And (O people!) your Companion is not possessed; and without doubt he saw him in the clear horizon. Neither does he withhold grudgingly a knowledge of the Unseen. [Surah 81:19-24]

JESUS

But after he [Joseph] had considered this, an angel of the Lord appeared to him in a dream and said, "Joseph son of David, do not be afraid to take Mary home as your wife, because what is conceived in her is from the Holy Spirit. 21She will give birth to a son, and you are to give him the name Jesus, because he will save his people from their sins." 22All this took place to fulfill what the Lord had said through the prophet: 23"The virgin will be with child and will give birth to a son, and they will call him Immanuel"—which means, "God with us." [Matthew 1:20-23]

"I [Jesus] and the Father are one." [John 10:30]

Anyone who has seen me has seen the Father. [John 14:1]

For there are three that bear witness in heaven: The Father, the Word, and the Holy Spirit; and these three are one. [I John 5:7]

22. Heaven-Paradise

ALLAH

23-But those who believe and work deeds of righteousness - to them shall We give a Home in Heaven, lofty mansions beneath which flow rivers. [Surah 29:58]

In Gardens of Felicity, facing each other on raised couches. Round will be passed to them a Cup from a clear-flowing fountain, Crystal-white, of a taste delicious to those who drink. Free from headlines; nor will they suffer intoxication. And besides them will be chaste women [virgins], restraining their glances, with big eyes (of wonder and beauty). [Surah 37:48]

Gardens of Eternity, whose doors will (ever) be open to them; Therein will they recline (at ease): Therein can they call (at pleasure) for fruit in abundance, and (delicious) drink; And beside them will be chaste women restraining their glances, (companions) of equal age. [Surah 38:50-52]

Among Gardens and Springs, dressed in fine silk and in rich brocade, they will face each other. ; and We shall join them to Companions with beautiful, big, and lustrous eyes. ["Surah 44:52-54]

As to the Righteous, they will be in Gardens, and in Happiness. "Eat and drink ye, with profit and health, because of your (good) deeds." They will recline (with ease) on couches (of dignity) arranged in ranks; and We shall join them to maidens with beautiful big and lustrous eyes. [Surah 52:17-20]

In them will be (maidens), chaste, restraining their glances, whom no man or Jinn before them has touched. [Surah 55:56]

And on couches (of Dignity), raised high. We have created (their Companions) of special creation. And made them virgin-pure (and undefiled) – Loving (by nature), equal in age. [Surah 56:34-37]

Surely, for the Righteous there will be a fulfillment of (the Heart's) desires; Gardens enclosed, and Grapevines; Maidens of Equal Age. [Surah 78:31-33]

JESUS

"Do not let your hearts be troubled. Trust in God; trust also in me. 2In my Father's house are many rooms [mansions]; if it were not so, I would have told you. I am going there to prepare a place for you. 3And if I go and prepare a place for you, I will come back and take you to be with me that you also may be where I am. 4You know the way to the place where I am going." [John 14:1-4]

So will it be with the resurrection of the dead.... it is sown a natural body; it is raised a spiritual body. [I Corinthians 15:42, 44]

After this I looked and there before me was a great multitude that no one could count, from every nation, tribe, people and language, standing before the throne and in front of the Lamb. They were wearing white robes and were holding palm branches in their hands. Therefore, they are before the throne of God and serve him day and night in his temple; and he who sits on the throne will spread his tent over them. Never again will they hunger; never again will they thirst. The sun will not beat upon them, nor any scorching heat. For the Lamb at the center of the throne will be their shepherd; he will lead them to springs of living water. And God will wipe away every tear from their eyes. [Revelation 7:9,15-17]

After this I heard what sounded like the roar of a great multitude in heaven shouting: "Hallelujah! Salvation and glory and power belong to our God, "Praise our God, all you his servants, you who fear him, both small and great!"

6Then I heard what sounded like a great multitude, like the roar of rushing waters and like loud peals of thunder, shouting: "Hallelujah! For our Lord God Almighty reigns. 7Let us rejoice and be glad and give him glory! [Revelation 19:1, 5-7]

23. First and Last

ALLAH

To Him belongs the dominion of the heavens and the earth; it is He Who gives life and Death; and He has Power over all things. He is the First and the Last, the Evident and the Immanent: and He has full knowledge of all things. [Surah 57:2-3]

JESUS

Jesus Christ, who is the faithful witness, the firstborn from the dead, and the ruler of the kings of the earth. To him who loves us and has freed us from our sins by his blood and has made us to be a kingdom of priests to serve God the Father ~ to him be glory and power for ever and ever! Amen. Look, he is coming with the clouds, and every eye will see him, even those who pierced him; and all the peoples of the earth will mourn because of him. So shall it be! Amen. "I am the Alpha and the Omega," says the Lord God, "who is and who was, and who is to come, the Almighty."

24. Prayer

ALLAH

Stand (to prayer) by night, but not all night – Half of it – or a little less, or a little more; and recite the Qur'an in slow, measured rhythmic tones. [Surah 73:2]

JESUS

And when you pray, do not use vain repetitions as the heathen do. For they think that they will be heard for their many words. [Matthew 6:7]

9"This, then, is how you should pray:
" 'Our Father in heaven, hallowed be your name,
10your kingdom come, your will be done on earth as it is in heaven.
11Give us today our daily bread.
12Forgive us our debts, as we also have forgiven our debtors.
13And lead us not into temptation, but deliver us from the evil one'
14For if you forgive men when they sin against you, your heavenly Father will also forgive you. [Matthew 6:8-14]

25. The Poor

ALLAH

27-And they feed, for the love of Allah, the indigent, the orphans, and the captive – (Saying), "We feed you for the sake of Allah alone; no reward do we desire from you, nor thanks. We only fear a Day of distressful Wrath from the side of our Lord." [Surah 76:8-10]

JESUS

Religion that God our Father accepts as pure and faultless is this: to look after orphans and widows in their distress and to keep oneself from being polluted by the world. [James 1:27]

"For I [Jesus] was hungry and you gave me something to eat, I was thirsty and you gave me something to drink, I was a stranger and you invited me in, 36I needed clothes and you clothed me, I was sick and you looked after me, I was in prison and you came to visit me.' 37"Then the righteous will answer him, 'Lord, when did we see you hungry and feed you, or thirsty and give you something to drink? 38When did we see you a stranger and invite you in, or needing clothes and clothe you? 39When did we see you sick or in prison and go to visit you?' 40"The King will reply, 'I tell you the truth, whatever you did for one of the least of these brothers of mine, you did for me.' [Matthew 25:35-40]

26. Slaves or Children?

ALLAH

And when My slaves ask you (O Muhammad) concerning Me, then (answer them), I am indeed near (to them by My Knowledge). I respond to the invocations of the supplicant when he calls on Me (without any mediator or intercessor). So let them obey Me and believe in Me, so that they may be led aright. [Surah 2:186]

And of mankind is he who would sell himself, seeking the Pleasure of Allah. And Allah is full of Kindness to (His) slaves. [Surah 2:207]

And Allah warns you against Himself (His punishment) and Allah is full of kindness to (His) slaves. [Surah 3:30]

And certainly, Allah is never unjust to (His) slaves. [Surah 3:182]

He is the Irresistible, (Supreme) over His slaves, and He sends guardians (angels guarding and writing all of one's good and bad deeds) over you, until when death approaches one of you, Our Messengers (angel of death and his assistants) take his soul, and they never neglect their duty. [Surah 6:61]

Know they not that Allah accepts repentance from His slaves and takes the Sadaqat (alms, charity), and that Allah Alone is the One Who forgives and accepts repentance, Most Merciful? [Surah 9:104]

Declare (O Muhammad) unto My slaves, that truly, I am the Oft-Forgiving, the Most-Merciful. [Surah 15:49]

And say to My slaves (i.e. the true believers of Islamic Monotheism) that they should (only) say those words that are the best.. [Surah 17:53]

That is because of what your hands have sent forth, and verily, Allah is not unjust to (His) slaves. [Surah 22:10]

And put your trust (O Muhammad) in the Ever Living One Who dies not, and glorify His Praises, and Sufficient is He as the All-Knower of the sins of His slaves. [Surah 25:58]

O My slaves who believe! Certainly, spacious is My earth. Therefore worship Me." [Surah 29:56]

"We would have indeed been the chosen slaves of Allah (true believers of Islamic Monotheism)!" [Surah 37:16]

"And you will remember what I am telling you, and my affair I leave it to Allah. Verily, Allah is the All-Seer of (His) slaves." [Surah 40:44]

Allah is very Gracious and Kind to His slaves. He gives provisions to whom He wills. And He is the All-Strong, the All-Mighty. [Surah 42:19]

Should not He Who has created know? And He is the Most Kind and Courteous (to His slaves), All-Aware (of everything). [Surah 67:14]

A spring wherefrom the slaves of Allah will drink, causing it to gush forth abundantly. [Surah 76:6]

JESUS

Blessed are the peacemakers, for they will be called sons of

God. [Matthew 5:9]

But I tell you: Love your enemies and pray for those who persecute you, 45that you may be sons of your Father in heaven. [Matthew 5:44]

But love your enemies, do good to them, and lend to them without expecting to get anything back. Then your reward will be great, and you will be sons of the Most High, because he is kind to the ungrateful and wicked. 36Be merciful, just as your Father is merciful. [Luke 6:35-36]

...because those who are led by the Spirit of God are sons of God. [Romans 8:14]

For you did not receive a spirit that makes you a slave again to fear, but you received the Spirit of sonship. And by him we cry, "Abba, Father." [Romans 8:15]

The Spirit himself testifies with our spirit that we are God's children. [Romans 8:16]

Now if we are children, then we are heirs—heirs of God and co-heirs with Christ, if indeed we share in his sufferings in order that we may also share in his glory. [Romans 8:17]

Praise be to the God and Father of our Lord Jesus Christ, who has blessed us in the heavenly realms with every spiritual blessing in Christ. 4For he chose us in him before the creation of the world to be holy and blameless in his sight. In love 5he predestined us to be adopted as his sons through Jesus Christ, in accordance with his pleasure and will— 6to the praise of his glorious grace, which he has freely given us in the One he loves. [Ephesians 1:3-6]

Be imitators of God, therefore, as dearly loved children 2and live a life of love, just as Christ loved us and gave himself up for us as a fragrant offering and sacrifice to God. [Ephesians 5:1]

For you were once darkness, but now you are light in the Lord. Live as children of light. [Ephesians 5:8]

No one who is born of God will continue to sin, because God's seed remains in him; he cannot go on sinning, because he has been born of God. [I John 3:9]

This is how we know who the children of God are and who the children of the devil are: Anyone who does not do what is right is not a child of God; nor is anyone who does not love his brother. [I John 3:10]

You are all sons of God through faith in Christ Jesus, 27for all of you who were baptized into Christ have clothed yourselves with Christ. 28There is neither Jew nor Greek, slave nor free, male nor female, for you are all one in Christ Jesus. [Galatians 3:26-27]

27. Questioning the Scriptures

ALLAH

O ye who believe! Ask not questions about things which, if made plain to you, may cause you trouble. Some people before you did ask such questions, and on that account lost their faith. [Surah 5:101-102]

JESUS

These were more noble than those in [another city], in that they received the word with all readiness of mind, and searched the scriptures daily, whether those things were so. [Acts 17:11]

28. Who Created Death?

ALLAH

Verily, Allah! Unto Him belongs the dominion of the heavens and the earth, He gives life and He causes Death. And besides Allah you have neither any Wali (protector or guardian) nor any helper. (Surah 9:116)

And that it is He (Allah) Who causes Death and gives life. (Surah 53:44)

He (Allah) Who created Death and Life, that He may try which of you is best in deed: and He is the Exalted in Might, Oft-Forgiving; (Surah 67:2)

JESUS

The devil...was a murderer from the beginning. (John 8:44)

Since the children have flesh and blood, he [Jesus] too shared in their humanity so that by his death he might break the power of him who holds the power of death—that is, the devil. (Hebrews 2:14)

Be alert and of sober mind. Your enemy the devil prowls around like a roaring lion looking for someone to devour. (I Peter 5:8)

This grace was given us in Christ Jesus before the beginning of time, but it has now been revealed through the appearing of our Savior, Christ Jesus, who has destroyed death. (II Timothy 1:9-10)

Then death and Hades were thrown into the lake of fire. The lake of fire is the second death. (Revelation 20:14)

29. How Long Sins Are Forgiven

ALLAH

But if they cease, Allah is oft-forgiving, Most Merciful. [Surah 2:192] (Also found in 84 other surahs in chapters 2-12, 14-17, 24-25, 27-28, 33-35, 39, 41-42, 46, 48-49, 57-58, 60, 64, 66-67, 61, 73, 85.)

We shall set up scales of justice for the Day of Judgment, so that not a soul will be dealt with unjustly in the least, and if there be (no more than) the weight of a mustard seed, We will bring it (to account): and enough are We to take account. [Surah 21:47]

Behold, two (guardian angels) appointed to learn (his doings) learn (and noted them), one sitting on the right and one on the left. Not a word does he utter but there is a sentinel by him, ready (to note it). [Surah 50:17-18]

We sent aforetime our apostles with Clear Signs and sent down with them the Book and the Balance (of Right and Wrong), that men may stand forth in justice. [Surah 57:25]

Then shall anyone who has done an atom's weight of good, see it! And anyone who has done an atom's weight of evil, shall see it. [Surah 99:7-8]

Those who believe and work righteous deeds, from them shall We blot out all evil (that may be) in them, and We shall reward them according to the best of their deeds. [Surah 29:7]

If any one does a righteous deed, it ensures to the benefit of his own soul; if he does evil, it works against (his own soul). [Surah 45:15]

Then he whose balance (of good deeds) will be (found) heavy, will be in a Life of good pleasure and satisfaction. But he whose balance (of good deeds) will be (found) light – Will have his home in a (bottomless) Pit. And what will explain to you what this is? (It is) a Fire blazing fiercely! [Surah 101:6-10]

JESUS

And you also were included in Christ when you heard the message of truth, the gospel of your salvation. When you believed, you were marked in him with a seal, the promised Holy Spirit, who is a deposit guaranteeing our inheritance [Ephesians 1:13-14]

Having been buried with him in baptism, in which you were also raised with him through your faith in the working of God, who raised him from the dead. When you were dead in your sins...God made you alive with Christ. He forgave us all our sins. [Colossians 2:12-13]

For you died, and your life is now hidden with Christ in God. When Christ, who is your life, appears (on the day of Judgment), then you also will appear with him in glory. [Colossians 3:3-4]

For I will forgive their wickedness and will remember their sins no more." [Hebrews 8:12]

How much more, then, will the blood of Christ, who through the eternal Spirit offered himself unblemished to God, cleanse our consciences from acts that lead to death, so that we may serve the living God!

For this reason, Christ is the mediator of a new covenant, that those who are called may receive the promised eternal inheritance—now that he has died as a ransom to set them free from the sins committed under the first covenant. [Hebrews 9:14-15]

"Their sins and lawless acts I will remember no more." [Hebrews 10:17]

This is how we know that we live in him and he in us: He has given us of his Spirit. And we have seen and testify that the Father has sent his Son to be the Savior of the world. If anyone acknowledges that Jesus is the Son of God, God lives in them and they in God. And so we know and rely on the love God has for us. God is love. Whoever lives in love lives in God, and God in them. This is how love is made complete among us so that we will have confidence on the day of judgment: In this world we are like Jesus. 18 There is no fear in love. [I John 4:13-18]

30. A Few Calculations

QURAN
(6236 verses)

95 times mentioned Hell
216 times mentioned Fire of Punishment
59 times mentioned Save, Salvation, Savior
104 times mentioned Loves/Love
93 times mentioned Fight (literal)
51 times mentioned Enemy/Enemies (mostly to fight)
140 times mentioned Judgment
192 times mentioned Unbelievers/Unbelief
31 times mentioned Hypocrites
142 times mentioned Command
0 times mentioned Children/Sons of God
112 times mentioned Slaves of God

INJIL (N.T.) of the BIBLE
(7957 verses)

22 times mentioned Hell
40 times mentioned Fire of Punishment
189 times mentioned Save, Salvation, Savior
147 times mentioned Love/Loves
15 times mentioned Fight (spiritual)
30 times mentioned Enemy/Enemies (mostly to love)
66 times mentioned Judgment
22 times mentioned Unbelievers/Unbelief
18 times mentioned Hypocrites
47 times mentioned Command
23 times mentioned God's Children
1 times mentioned God's Slaves

31. Names
(Alphabetic, but in Arabic number order)

99 NAMES OF ALLAH

23. Abaser, by his will to destroy or raise
69. Able, Powerful
80. Accepter of repentance, forgives as he will
63. Alive, not soul, flesh or blood
35. All-Forgiving
81. Avenger, punisher of enemies
42. Beneficient, sublime
17. Bestower, generous, giving without any return
85. Bounty and majesty deserves to be exalted, not denied
02. Compassionate
10. Compeller whose will is always done
83. Compassionate, merciful
58. Counter, reckoner
12. Creator from non-existence to existence
09. Defeater who is strong, never defeated
72. Delayer of what he wills
62. Destroyer, Creator of Death
26. Dishonorer, humiliator of who he will
91. Distresser, harms who he will to benefit who he will
01. Divinity, Godhead
70. Dominant, nothing withheld from
89. Enricher, satisfies needs of creatures
86. Equitable, Just
68. Eternal, independent, master
96. Everlasting
78. Exalted, clear from attributes of his creations (but see below)
71. Expediter, promoter. Makes ahead what he wills,

delays what he wills
    14. Fashioner, forms his creatures in different pictures
    55. Firm one, never tires
    73. First, with no beginning
    33. Forbearing, delays punishment to give chance to repent
    15. Forgiver of his slaves' sins again and again
    56. Friend, protector, supporter
    87. Gatherer on Day of Judgment
    43. Generous, bountiful
    49. Glorious more than all
    77. Governor, owns and manages
    38. Greater than everything, most great
    07. Guardian of Faith, the only God
    40. Guardian, feeder, maintainer, sustainer
    94. Guide
    27. Hearing all, without an ear (human characteristic)
    76. Hidden
    51. Hidden from nothing, witness to everything
    05. Holy, pure from imperfection
    24. Honored or Degrader of who he will
    95. Incomparable, created without any preceding example
    19. Judge, opener of the closed world & religious matters
    30. Just One
    04. King, Sovereign Lord
    32. Knower of truth of things, Aware
    20. Knowing all
    74. Last, without end
    93. Light, one who guides
    48. Loves his believing slaves and they love him in peace
    11. Majestic with no attributes of his creatures
{Contradicted since Allah sees, hears, gets angry, etc.}
    03. Merciful
    67. One
    59. Originator of humans
    84. Owner of sovereignty, controls dominions & gives dominions to who he will
    82. Pardoner, forgiver

98. Path is right, guides us to it
99. Patient, does not quickly punish
65. Perceiver, Richer and never poor
57. Praiseworthy
39. Preserver, protector of whoever he wills
90. Preventer, withholder
75. Proven, manifest, exists without place or body
92. Propitious, harms who he will
34. Pure from all imperfection, Great One
97. Remains forever, supreme inheritor, heir
60. Reproducer, brings back after death
61. Restorer of life, takes living human from semen that does not have a soul and gives the souls back to their old bodies on resurrection day; makes hearts alive by light of knowledge
50. Resurrector from death to reward or punishment
36. Rewards much from gratitude for a little obedience
79. Righteous, merciful, source of goodness
29. Ruler & Judge; his judgment is his Word
41. Satisfier, One who Reckons
28. Seeing all without a pupil (a human characteristic)
64. Self-subsisting, never ending
88. Self-sufficient, does not need his creation
06. Slaves, not children. Source of peace, free from imperfection
54. Strong with complete power
16. Subduer, dominator
37. Sublime, Most High, free of attributes of his creatures (but see above)
31. Subtle one who is gracious to his slaves
18. Sustainer and provider
22. Sustenance constrictor or sustainer with mercy
21. Sustenance withholder or expander with mercy
52. True, truly exists
53. Trustee, one relied upon
13. Turner and evolver of entities
66. Unique, without a partner
46. Vast, all-embracing, all knowing

44. Watcher, all-knowing
47. Wise, Judge of judges, correct
08. Witnesses deeds of his creatures, protector

153 NAMES OF THE GOD OF THE BIBLE

ALL THE ABOVE EXCEPT:

62. Destroyer, Creator of Death – This is the name of Satan in the Bible

92. Propitious, harms who he will – Jesus is propitious and saves

61. At resurrection, puts souls back in their old bodies – At resurrection, gives them spiritual bodies

06. Worshipers are his slaves – Worshippers no longer slaves

37. Free of attributes of his creatures – Humans created in God's image

ADDITIONAL NAMES:
100. Abba Father
101. Advocate
102. Almighty
103. Amen
104. Ancient of Days
105. Anointed One
106. Author of Life
107. Author of Faith
108. Bread of Life
109. Christ the Lord
110. Comforter
111. Commander
112. Consolation
113. Counselor
114. Deliverer
115. Desire of All Nations
116. Door

117. Faithful and True
118. Father everlasting
119. Foundation
120. Friend of Sinners
121. Gentle Whisper
122. Holy Spirit
123. Hope
124. Horn of Salvation
125. King f kings, King of the Ages
126. LIFE
127. Like an eagle
128. Lily of the Valley
129. Lion
130. Living Stone
131. Living Water
132. Lord of lords, Lord of Glory, Lord of Hosts
133. Lord of our Righteousness
134. **LOVE**
135. Master
136. Messiah
137. Mighty God, Mighty One
138. Morning Star
139. Peace, Prince of Peace
140. Potter
141. Purifier
142. Redeemer
143. Rock, Rock of Salvation
144 Shepherd of our Souls
145. Shield
146. Stone
147. Sun of Righteousness
148. Teacher
149. TRUTH
150. Vine
151. Way
152. Wonderful
153. **WORD**

32. There is One God

Despite what Muslims may have heard about Christians, God is One, not many. When you speak into a tape recorder and your voice then comes out of that machine for other people to hear, that doesn't make you two. You are still one; you have just chosen to put your voice in something where you can be heard by more people or people far away. That tape recording is just another form of you.

God is One, and yet he revealed a part of himself in a burning tree to Moses just like you revealed a part of yourself in the tape recorder. Does that mean there were two Gods ~ one in heaven and one in the tree? No. God can reveal himself in different things if he wants to.

Today, God has his Word on paper and ink in a holy Book. He has made his words visible to us in physical form. He is still not many Gods ~ one in heaven and thousands in his holy Books around the world. He is still one God.

To say "God needs no partners" is the same as denying we have a body, and declaring, "My mind needs no body". We need our body to show others what we are like. True, God doesn't need a body, but mankind, who dwells in the bodies he created for our minds to use, needed to see for themselves what God is like. So God revealed himself in a body for a little while.

God can put his voice in a human being and that human say the exact words of God just like you can put your voice in a tape recorder and that recorder say the exact words of you. You can also put both your voice and body in a movie. God is still not two any more than you become two.

God can put his words in a tree (as with Moses), in holy books (with paper and ink), and a human body (as with Jesus). God is still one.

To say "God has no son" is the same as saying "God has no hands" or "God has no eyes". Even the Qur'an speaks of God having hands and eyes. Would it be fair to accuse Muslims of believing God has them in the human sense? Of course not, for God is a spirit. It is unfair to accuse Christians of believing God had to have a wife so he could have a son in the human way like we do. That is a terrible idea. God's Son is God's Word.

Jesus is often called "the Word" or "God's Word". God watches people, but not with literal eyes the way we have them. In the same way, God can have a "son," but not in the literal sense that we do. John 1:1-3,14 in the Bible explains, "In the beginning was the Word, and THE WORD WAS WITH GOD and THE WORD WAS GOD....The Word became flesh and made his dwelling among us." Why? Because we needed to know how God would act with part of him in a human body.

You have an eternal mind that is in your body right now. That body says and does things to show people what is in your mind. But it is just temporary. When your body dies, you will live on because your body is not the real you. Your mind, your eternal mind, is the real you. In the same way, when God was in Jesus' body, that body was not God. The mind, the spirit, the heart and soul in that body was God.

We can be children of God. But it would be foolish to say Christians believe God had lots of wives and we became his children the way humans do. God "adopts" us and makes us his children. It is a spiritual thing, and wonderful.

Why would Jesus be called the only begotten Son of God, if he was not a son created in the literal way that we have sons? You have thoughts and those thoughts have existed as long as you have. But you still created those thoughts. When your thoughts become hearable or seeable, people call that your "brain child". In that same sense, Jesus was God's "brain child" ~ God's thoughts in hearable and seeable form. God was in Jesus in the same way that you are in a tape recorder or in a movie. You are still one and God is still one.

33. Jesus' Life Before He Was "Born"

Some people ask, "You Christians claim Jesus was God and God is one. In that case, there was no God before Jesus was born. In fact, when Jesus died on the cross, once again there was no God."

These are good thoughts. They seem to come from logic. But this logic is based on partial knowledge. A person has to look at the facts.

In the *Qur'an*, it says God appeared to Moses in a burning tree, and spoke out of that burning tree. (The Bible has the same story, except it was a burning bush.) Here is the *Qur'an* version:

When he saw a fire, he said to his family: "Wait! Verily, I have seen a fire; perhaps I can bring you some burning brand there from, or **find some guidance at the fire.**" And when he came to it (the fire), he was called by name: "O Musa (Moses)! **"Verily I am your Lord!** So take off your shoes; you are in the sacred valley, Tuwa. (Surah 20:10-12)

(Remember) when Musa (Moses) said to his household: "Verily I have seen a fire; I will bring you from there some information, or I will bring you a burning brand, that you may warm yourselves." But when he came to it, he was called: "**Blessed is whosoever is in the fire,** and whosoever is round about it! And glorified be Allah, the Lord of the 'Alamin (mankind, jinn and all that exists). "O Musa (Moses)! **Verily it is I, Allah, the All-Mighty,** the All-Wise. (Surah 27:7-9).

Then, when Musa (Moses) had fulfilled the term, and was traveling with his family, he saw a fire in the direction of Tur (Mount). He said to his family: "Wait, I have seen a fire; perhaps I may bring you from there some information, or a burning fire-brand that you may warm yourselves." So when he reached it **(the fire), he was called** from the right side of the valley, in the blessed place, **from the tree: "O Musa (Moses)! Verily I am Allah.** (Surah 28:29-30)

Would it have made sense for the other trees to say, "God

never entered us and spoke out of us, so we do not believe God really entered and spoke out of that other tree"? Furthermore, would it make sense to say that before that tree was planted, God did not exist; and after that tree died and was blown away, God did not exist?

We could ask the same questions about the fire. Should all other flames of fire say that, since God did not speak out of them, God did not speak out of that fire either? Should all other flames of fire say that, before that particular flame of fire came into being, God did not exist; and after that particular flame of fire was blown out, God went out of existence?

If your answer to both questions is "No, it wouldn't make sense," then it does not make sense to deny God put his words in the human body of Jesus just because he didn't put his words in your human body or any other human body.

JESUS ALWAYS EXISTED

John 1:1-3, in the New Testament half of the Bible, says, Jesus is God: "In the beginning was the Word, and the **Word was with God, and the Word was God**. He was with God in the beginning. He was with God in the beginning. Through him all things were made [spoken into existence]; without him nothing was made that has been made."

In John 17:5, Jesus said he had glory with God before the world began.

King Solomon, the son of David, wrote this about Jesus, the Word: "The Lord brought me forth [possessed me] as the **first of his works before his deeds** of old; **I was appointed from eternity,** from the beginning, before the world began. When there were no oceans, I was given birth [brought forth], when there were no springs abounding with water; before the mountains were settled in place, before the hills, I was given birth [brought forth], before he made the earth or its fields or any of the dust of the world" (Proverbs 8:22-26).

"**For by him all things were created**: things in heaven and on earth, visible and invisible....**He is before all things**, and in him all things hold together. And he is the head of the body, the church; he is the beginning and the firstborn from among the dead" (Colossians 1:16-18).

"Christ Jesus who, being in **very nature God**...made himself nothing, taking the very nature of a servant, being made in human likeness and **being found in appearance as a man**" (Philippians 2:5-8).

"**He appeared in a body**, was vindicated by the Spirit, was seen by angels, was preached among the nations, was believed on in the world, was taken up in glory" (1st Timothy 3:16)

"The Son is the radiance of **God's glory and the exact representation of his being**, sustaining all things by his powerful Word. After he provided purification for sins, he sat down at the right hand of the Majesty in heaven ....About the **Son he says, 'Your throne, O God**, will last forever and ever." (Hebrews 1:3, 8).

"He was **foreknown before the foundation of the world**, but has appeared" (1st Peter 1:20)

"If anyone acknowledges that Jesus is the Son of God, **God lives in him and he in God**" (1st John 4:15).

Well, how can Jesus be eternal and be created too? Your mind has always existed. Your mind is the father of your words. Any time God thought in Words, that was Jesus before he became Jesus. Any time Jesus spoke in Words, that was Jesus before he became Jesus

Therefore, whenever Jesus said he had to do the will of his Father, he was saying the Words had to obey the Mind.

This also assures us there is only one Word of God.

WHAT JESUS WAS

In the New Testament of the Bible (written for Christians), Jesus' apostle John said, "In the beginning was the Word, and the

Word was with God, and the Word was God. He was with God in the beginning. **The Word became flesh** and made his dwelling among us. We have seen his glory, the glory of the One and Only [there is only one Word of God] who came from the Father, full of grace and truth" (John 1:1 & 14).

This same apostle wrote in the very last book of the Bible this: "**His name is the Word of God**....On his robe and on his thigh he has this name written: King of kings and Lord of lords" (Revelation 19:13 & 16).

WHENEVER GOD SPOKE, THAT WAS JESUS

To understand the Word, it helps to understand the Spirit, for we run into the term Holy Son and Holy Spirit both. You have a mind that is the originator of all things you say and do. You have a spirit within you that keeps you alive; when someone dies, we say their spirit left them. And we've already discussed words.

The part God's Spirit plays is brought out in Genesis 1:1-2 that says, "In the beginning God created the heavens and the earth. Now the earth was formless and empty, darkness was over the surface of the deep, and the Spirit of God was hovering over the waters." This is followed in the rest of the chapter with God saying, "Let there be" and something came into existence.

Here we have God, the Mind, speaking something into existence (Jesus, the Word), and God the Spirit making it happen. (For a further study of the Holy Spirit, I have *The Holy Spirit: 592 Verses Examined*, which can be purchased from any online bookseller or in discount paperback at The Bible House, Searcy, Arkansas.)

JESUS' APPEARANCES

We have instances when God appeared as a man, but it is

always explained that the man was God who had temporarily materialized.

Whenever **God's Angel** is referred to, that is Jesus. He led the Israelites across the wilderness between Egypt and the future Palestine. God told the Israelites, "Pay attention to him and listen to what he says. Do not rebel against him, for he will not forgive your rebellion, since my name is in him....**My angel** will go ahead of you" (Exodus 23:21-23).

Jesus is referred to as God's Angel also in the last book of the Bible, Revelation. "The revelation of Jesus Christ which God gave him...He made it known by sending his angel [Jesus] to his servant John. "(See Revelation 1:1-2.)

Furthermore, whenever you read "The Angel of the Lord" (not **an** angel, but **The** Angel), in the Old Testament half of the Bible, that is Jesus. Remember, angel simply means messenger. The passages referring to The Angel always explain that it is God speaking; that is, God the Word speaking ~ Jesus.

Abraham
c. 2054 BC

Abraham waited a long time to have a son. When he was finally born, he was a miracle baby, for Abraham was now one hundred years old, and his wife was ninety years old. Later, probably when Isaac was a teenager, God told Abraham to sacrifice his only begotten son to him.

(Some ask why Abraham's first-born, Ishmael, wasn't considered his begotten son. Ishmael was the son of a slave woman, Hagar, and that made Ishmael a slave too. He was not legally recognized as a son.)

In the Bible account of the sacrifice, it says, "But **The Angel of the Lord** called out to him from heaven, 'Do not lay a hand on the boy. Now I know that you fear **God,** because you **have not withheld from me** your son, your only son' " (Genesis 22:11-12).

Then "The **Angel of the Lord** called to Abraham from heaven a second time and said, 'I swear by **myself**, declares **the Lord,** that, because you have not withheld your son, your only son, I will surely bless you..." (Genesis 22:15-17a).

WHENEVER GOD MATERIALIZED, THAT WAS JESUS

Abraham
2067 BC

When Abraham was ninety-nine years old, "**The Lord appeared** to Abraham....Abraham looked up and saw **three men** standing nearby....He said, 'If I have found favor in your eyes, my Lord, do not pass your servant by....Then **the Lord said**, "I will return to you about this time next year, and Sarah your wife will have a son....Is anything too hard for the Lord?'" (See Genesis 18:1-14.) We see here that Jesus announced the birth of Isaac.

Abraham
2067 BC

There were some cities that were very evil and **God decided** to destroy them completely. "When the men got up to leave, they looked down toward Sodom....Then the **Lord said**, 'Shall I hide from Abraham what I am about to do?'...Then **the Lord said**, 'The outcry against Sodom and Gomorrah is so great and their sin so grievous'...The [three] men turned away and went toward Sodom, but Abraham approached **him** and said: 'Will you sweep away the righteous with the wicked? What if there are fifty righteous people in the city?...The **Lord said**, 'If I find fifty righteous people in the city of Sodom, **I will spare** the whole place for heir sake'...When the **Lord had finished speaking** with Abraham, he left and Abraham returned home. The two angels arrived at Sodom in the evening....So, when **God**

destroyed the cities of the plain, he remembered Abraham." (Genesis 18:16 – 19:1, 29). We see here that Jesus materialized in the form of one of the three men who visited Abraham. When the Lord appeared to Abraham, that was who we would later identify as Jesus.

Hagar
2064 BC

Sarah, the wife of Abraham, could not bear him children. So, according to the custom 4000 years ago, Sarah suggested her husband mate with her Egyptian slave, Hagar, so she could be a surrogate mother for a child for Sarah. But, when Hagan became pregnant, she began acting ugly toward Sarah and taunting her. So Sarah treated Hagar the same way Hagar had treated her, and Hagar ran away.

"**The Angel of the Lord** found her and told her, 'Go back to your mistress and submit to her." He also told her she would have a son and was to name him Ishmael. Hagar replied, "**You are the God** who sees me. I have now seen the One who sees me." (See Genesis 16:9-13.)

Jacob
1906 BC

Years later, Jacob returned home. By this time, he had two wives and twelve sons. He neared his homeland. "So Jacob was left alone, and **the man** wrestled with him till daybreak.....Then the man said, 'Let me go, for it is daybreak.' But Jacob replied, 'I will not let you go unless you bless me....Then the man said, Your name will no longer be Jacob, but Israel, because you have struggled with **God** and with men and have overcome....So Jacob called the place Peniel, saying, 'It is because I **saw God face to face**, and yet my life was spared'" (Genesis 32:24-30). Jacob was about to enter a hostile land that God was giving him. That night, when he wrestled all night, he proved he was a man who could stick with something longer than other men could. He had wrestled with a physical manifestation of God, Jesus.

Aaron & Miriam
1445 BC

Jacob, now called Israel, had a son, Joseph who started out as a slave in Egypt and eventually became next to Pharaoh in importance. He brought his father and brothers to be with him in Egypt. But they did not return home. They stayed until the Egyptians turned them into slaves. They were slaves 400 years. Then Moses led them out of their slavery. There were over three million in this family by now and they were called Israelites. Moses had an older sister, Miriam, and older brother, Aaron. Moses led these former slaves for forty years. At one point, his brother and sister resented him being the leader and not them. So, God appeared to them to set them straight.

"Then the Lord came down in a pillar of cloud; he **stood** at the entrance to the tent and summoned Aaron and Miriam. When the two of them stepped forward, 6 he said, "Listen to my words: When there is a prophet among you, I, the Lord, reveal myself to them in visions, I speak to them in dreams. But this is not true of my servant Moses; he is faithful in all my house. With him I speak **face to face**, clearly and not in riddles; **he sees the form of the Lord**. Why then were you not afraid to speak against my servant Moses?" (Numbers 12:5-8). Notice, the Lord stood and explained that Moses always sees his face and form.

Balaam
1407 BC

A pagan prophet named Balaam wanted to prophesy against the Israelites. So, **"The Angel of the Lord** stood in the road to oppose him....the Lord opened Balaam's eyes and he saw The Angel of the Lord standing in the road with his sword drawn. So he bowed low and fell face down" (Numbers 22:22, 31). We know this was not just an ordinary angel because, when an ordinary angel was bowed down to, he said it was wrong. "Then the angel said to me....At this I fell down at this feet to worship him, but he said to me, 'Do not do it! I am a fellow servant" (Revelation 19:9-10). The same thing happened in Revelation 22:8 when John was again told not to bow down before an angel.

Joshua
1406 BC

After Moses died, Joshua took his place. As he led the people near Jericho, Joshua "saw a man standing in front of him with a drawn sword in his hand. The man said, " 'As **commander of the army of the Lord** I have now come.' Then Joshua **fell facedown** to the ground in reverence....The commander of the Lord's army replied, 'Take off your sandals, for the **place where you are standing is holy**' " (Joshua 5:13-15).

Joshua & Israelites
1375 BC

Shortly before Joshua died, **The Angel of the Lord** told the Israelites, "I brought you up out of Egypt and led you into the land I swore to give to your forefathers. I said I will never break **my covenant** with you." Angels did not make covenants with people; only God did.

Gideon
1169 BC

The Israelites settled in their land, but turned from God. Finally Gideon, a supreme judge over Israel was approached by God. "When **The Angel of the Lord** appeared to Gideon, he said,

'The Lord is with you....**The Lord answered**, "I will be with you.' " At the end of their conversation "The Angel of the Lord disappeared. When Gideon realized it was The Angel of the Lord, he exclaimed, 'Ah, sovereign Lord! I have seen the angel of the Lord face to face" (Judges 6:12-16, 21-22).

Samson's Parents
1090 BC

At a time when the Israelites were being ruled by their enemy because of their sin, **The Angel of the Lord appeared** to Manoah's wife. She told her husband, a man of God came to her who looked like an angel of God, very awesome (Judges 13:3, 6). He later appeared to both Manoah and his wife. Manoah offered to fix him a meal and he turned him down, but said he should prepare a burnt offering to the Lord. "Then Manoah inquired of **The Angel of the Lord**, 'What is your name, so we may honor you when your word comes true?' He replied, 'Why do you ask my name? It is beyond understanding' ". Then Manoah made the burnt offering to the Lord, and "as the flame blazed up from the altar toward heaven, **The Angel of the Lord** ascended in the flame...We are doomed to die, for we have **seen God**!" (Judges 13:12-22)

Elijah
858 BC

The prophet Elijah fled from the evil queen of the Israelites, Jezebel. While he was hiding, **The Angel of the Lord** touched him and told him to eat because he needed to go to the desert of Damascus. He hid in a cave, then "the word of the Lord came to him" (I Kings 19:7-9).

Shadrach, Meshach & Abednego

603 BC

Eventually, God allowed the Israelites to be taken captive to Babylon (today's Iraq). There were three godly Jews among them named Shadrach, Meshach and Abednego. They refused to bow down to a statue, so King Nebuchadnezzar ordered that they be thrown into a fiery furnace. "Then King Nebuchadnezzar leaped to his feet I amazement and asked his advisors, 'Weren't there three men that we tied up and threw into the fire…Look! **I see** four men walking around in the fire, unbound and unharmed, and the **fourth looks like a Son of God**' " (Daniel 3:24-25). Then he ordered the three men to come out of the fire, and they did. The fourth "man" disappeared.

SOMETIMES JESUS APPEARED IN AN OBJECT

A Stairway
1928 BC

After Jacob deceived his father, Isaac, and got the blessing of his older brother, Esau, he had to flee for his life. While on his way to another country, he had a vision of a stairway [ladder] coming down from heaven with angels ascending and descending on it (Genesis 28:12)

Centuries later, Jesus explained he was that stairway. He said, "Very truly I tell you, you will see 'heaven open, and the angels of God ascending and descending on' the Son of Man" (John 1:51).

A Burning Bush/Tree
1446 BC

The Israelites eventually went to Egypt because of a famine, but never returned home. Eventually they were turned into slaves by the Egyptians because they were another nationality that might try to take over their country. They were slaves 400 years. Then God appeared to Moses to tell him to lead them out of slavery. "There **The Angel of the Lord appeared** to him in flames of fire from within a bush....**God called** to him from within the bush...'Do not come any closer,' **God said.** 'Take off your sandals, for the place where you are standing is holy ground.'...**The Lord said,** 'I have indeed seen the misery of my people in Egypt. I have heard them crying out' " (Exodus 3:2-7).

A Pillar of Cloud &/Or Fire
1446 BC

The Israelites did not know where they were going because they had been slaves in Egypt 400 years. So God led them. "Then **The Angel of God**, who had been traveling in front of Israel's army, withdrew and went behind them. The **pillar of cloud** also moved from in front and stood behind them, coming between the armies of Egypt and Israel....During the last watch of the night, the **Lord** looked down from the **pillar of fire and cloud** at the Egyptian army and threw it into confusion. (See Exodus 14:19-20, 24.)

Later Jesus appeared in a cloud when Solomon finished building and dedicated the temple in Jerusalem. When the sacred ark (golden chest) of the covenant was brought into the temple and put in the Holy of Holies, as the priests were leaving the building through the Holy Place, a cloud filled the temple, "so that the priests could not stand to minister because of the **cloud**, for the **glory of the Lord** filled the house of the Lord" (I Kings 8:10-11). That cloud, too, was Jesus.

A Rock With Water
1407 BC

The Israelites were in the wilderness after they left Egypt and became thirsty. So God told Moses and his brother, Aaron (their high priest) to "speak to that rock before their eyes and it will pour out its water. You will bring water out of the rock for the community" Exodus 20:8).

In the New Testament half of the Bible, it says they all "drank the same spiritual drink; for they drank from the spiritual rock that accompanied them, and that rock was Christ" (I Corinthians 10:4). In fact, Jesus also said he was the water in John 4:14, also in the New Testament half of the Bible.

~~~~~

So, we see in the above that the Word of God (later known as Jesus) had a fairly busy life before he was born in the body of Jesus.

JESUS WAS THE VISIBLE IMAGE OF THE INVISIBLE GOD

The prophet Isaiah (peace be upon him), wrote that a child would be born some day who will be both the Son that is given and the Everlasting Father, and will be Mighty God (Isaiah 9:6).

When the angel, Gabriel, appeared to Joseph to explain that Mary was miraculously pregnant, he told Joseph "they will call him Immanuel, which means "God With Us". This had been prophesied centuries earlier when it was said, "Therefore the Lord himself will give you a sign: The virgin will be with child and will give birth to a son, and will call him Immanuel" (Isaiah 7:14).

"He is the image of the invisible God, the firstborn over all creation....For God was pleased to have all is fullness dwell in him" (Colossians 1:15, 19).

So, when God walked with Adam and Eve in the Garden of Eden (Genesis 3:8).

Philippians 2:5-8, explains this: "Your attitude should be the same as that of Christ Jesus who, being in very nature God, did not consider equality with God something to be grasped, but made himself nothing, taking the very nature of a servant, being made in human likeness. And being in appearance as a man, he humbled himself and became obedient to death—even death on a cross."

So, why did Jesus become the visible image of God by going into the body of a man? Hebrews 2:11-14, "Both the one who makes men holy [Jesus] and those who are made holy [Jesus' followers, Christians] are the same family. So Jesus is not ashamed to call them brothers.... 'Here am I, and the children God has given me.' Since the children have flesh and blood, he too shared in their humanity so that by his death he might destroy him who holds the power of death—that is, the devil."

34. Prophecies of Jesus Fulfilled In His Lifetime
(Some of Many)

1. PROPHECY c. 1420 BC - Genesis 22:15,18
"ABRAHAM....through your offspring all nations on earth will be blessed."
FULFILLED - Matthew 1:1
"A record of the genealogy of Jesus Christ the son of David, the son of ABRAHAM."

2. PROPHECY c. 1000 BC - *Psalm 89:3,4,27*
"*I have made a covenant with my chosen one, I have sworn to DAVID my servant, I will establish your line forever and make your throne firm through all generations....I will also appoint him my firstborn, the most exalted of the kings of the earth.*"
FULFILLED - *John 7:42*
"*Does not the Scripture say that the Christ will come from DAVID'S family and from Bethlehem, the town where David lived?*"

3. PROPHECY c. 530 BC - Daniel 9:24-27
"Seventy 'sevens' [490 years] are decreed for your people and your holy city [Jerusalem] to finish transgression [punishment]....and to anoint [crown] the most holy. Know and understand this: From the issuing of the decree to restore and rebuild Jerusalem until the Anointed One [priest-king], the ruler, comes, there will be seven 'sevens' [49 years] and sixty-two 'sevens' [+434 years = 483 years+]....After the sixty-two 'sevens,' [434 years] the Anointed One [priest-king] will be cut off and will have nothing....He will confirm a covenant with many for one 'seven' [+set of 7 years = 490 years]. In the middle of the 'seven' [3-1/2 years] he will put an end to sacrifice and offering" [sacrifice himself - Hebrews 10:3-5].
FULFILLED

['weeks' = years. 7 days in a week represent years.]
49 years + 434 years = 483 years

BC 457 city walls of Jerusalem rebuilt
AD +26 Jesus, at age 30, began to preach (Luke 3:23)
483 years
+ 7 years confirm [New] covenant [Testament]
*490 years

*But in middle of the 7 (3-1/2 yrs) will put an end to sacrificing [animal sacrifices]

Jesus preached 3-1/2 years, then was crucified, being the sacrificial Lamb of God (John 1:29, 18:28 & 19:16-18).

After that, sacrificing animals at the Temple became unnecessary (Hebrews 10:3-5).

4. PROPHECY c. 686 BC - *Micah 5:2*

"But you, BETHLEHEM Ephrathat, though you are small among the clans of Judah, out of you will come for me one who will be ruler over Israel, whose origins are from of old, from ancient times."

FULFILLED - *Matthew 2:3-5*

"When King Herod heard this, he was disturbed, and all Jerusalem with him. When he had called together all the people's chief priests and teachers of the law, he asked them where the Christ was to be born. 'In BETHLEHEM in Judea,' they replied, 'for this is what the prophet has written.'"

5. PROPHECY c. 600 BC - Jeremiah 31:15

"A voice is heard [way over] in Ramah, mourning and great [loud] weeping. Rachel [Isaac's Wife, Grandmother of 12 Tribes of Israel] WEEPING FOR HER CHILDREN and refusing to be comforted, because her children are no more."

FULFILLED - Matthew 2:16

"When Herod realized that he had been outwitted by the Magi, he was furious, and he gave orders to KILL ALL THE BOYS IN BETHLEHEM AND ITS VICINITY WHO WERE TWO YEARS OLD AND UNDER, in accordance with the time he had learned from the Magi."

6. PROPHECY *c. 700 BC - Hosea 11:1*
"*When Israel was a child, I loved him, and out of EGYPT I called my son.*"
FULFILLED - *Matthew 2:14-15*
"*So he [Joseph] got up, took the child [Jesus] and his mother [Mary] during the night and left for EGYPT where he stayed until the death of Herod.*"

7. PROPHECY c. 430 BC - Malachi 3:1
"See, I will SEND MY MESSENGER who will prepare the way before me. Then suddenly, the Lord you are seeking will come to his temple; the messenger of the covenant, whom you desire, will come."
FULFILLED - John 1:19, 29
"Now this was JOHN'S TESTIMONY when the Jews of Jerusalem sent priests and Levites to ask him who he was. He did not fail to confess, but confessed freely, 'I am not the Christ.' The next day John saw Jesus coming toward him and said, 'Lo, the Lamb of God, who takes away the sin of the world!' "

8. PROPHECY *c. 700 BC - Isaiah 40:3*
"*A voice of one calling: 'In the DESERT prepare the way for the Lord, make straight in the WILDERNESS a highway for our God.'* "
FULFILLED - *Matthew 3:4-5*
"*John's clothes were made of camel's hair, and he had a leather belt around this waist. His FOOD WAS LOCUSTS AND WILD HONEY. People went out to him from Jerusalem and all Judea and the whole region of the Jordan.*"

9. PROPHECY c. 700 BC - Isaiah 9:1-2, 7
"In the past he humbled the land of Zebulun and the land of Naphtali. In the future he will honor GALILEE of the Gentiles by the way of the sea, along the Jordan. The people walking in darkness have seen a great light, on those living in the land of the shadow of death, a light has dawned....Of the increase of his

government and peace there will be no end."
FULFILLED - Matthew 4:13
"Leaving Nazareth, he went and lived in Capernaum, which was by the lake in the area of Zebulun and Naphtali, to fulfill what was said through the prophet Isaiah, 'Land of Zebulun and land of Nephtali, the way to the sea, along the Jordan, GALILEE of the Gentiles ~ the people living in darkness have seen a great light, on those living in the land of the shadow of death a light has dawned.' From that time on Jesus began to preach, 'Repent, for the kingdom of heaven is near.' "

10. PROPHECY c. 700 BC - Isaiah 35:4-6
"Say to those with fearful hearts, 'Be strong, do not fear; your God will come, he will come with vengeance [against Satan]; with divine retribution he will come to save you.' Then will the eyes of the BLIND be opened, the ears of the DEAF unstopped. Then will the LAME leap like a deer, and the MUTE tongue shout for joy."
FULFILLED - John 20:30-31
"Jesus did many other MIRACULOUS SIGNS in the presence of his disciples, which are not recorded in this book. But these are written that you may believe that Jesus is the Christ, the Son of God, and that by believing you may have life in his name."

11. PROPHECY c. 1000 BC - Psalm 78:2
"I will open my mouth in PARABLES, I will utter hidden things, things from of old."
FULFILLED - Matthew 13:34
"Jesus spoke all these things to the crowd in PARABLES; he did not say anything to them without using a parable. "

12. PROPHECY c. 1000 BC - Psalm 69:8
"I am a stranger to my BROTHERS, an alien to my own mother's sons."
FULFILLED - John 7:5
"For even his own BROTHERS did not believe in him."

13. PROPHECY c. 1000 BC - Psalm 35:19; 69:4; Isaiah 49:7

"Let not those who hate me without reason maliciously wink the eye....Those who HATE ME WITHOUT REASON outnumber the hairs of my head....The Redeemer and Holy One of Israel ~ to him who was despised and abhorred by the nation, to the servant of rulers...the Lord, who is faithful, the Holy One of Israel, who has chosen you."

FULFILLED - John 15:24b-25

"But now they have seen these miracles and yet they have HATED BOTH ME AND MY FATHER. But this is to fulfill what is written in their Law, "They hated me without reason.""

14. PROPHECY c. 450 BC - Zechariah 9:9

"Rejoice greatly, O Daughter of Zion! Shout, Daughter of Jerusalem! See, your king comes to you, righteous and having salvation, gentle and riding on a donkey, on a colt, the FOAL OF A DONKEY."

FULFILLED - Matthew 21:7

"They brought the DONKEY AND THE COLT, placed their cloaks on them, and Jesus sat on them."

15. PROPHECY c. 1000 BC - Psalm 41:9

"Even my CLOSE FRIEND whom I trusted, he who shared my bread, has lifted up his heel AGAINST ME."

FULFILLED - Matthew 10:1-2,4; John 13:21,26

"He called his twelve disciples to him and gave them authority to drive out evil spirits and to heal every disease and sickness. These are the names of the twelve APOSTLES...AND JUDAS Iscariot, who betrayed him....After he had said this, Jesus was troubled in spirit and testified, 'I tell you the truth, one of you is going to BETRAY me...It is the one to whom I will give this piece of bread when I have dipped it in the dish. Then dipping the piece of bread, he gave it to Judas Iscariot....

16. PROPHECY c. 485 BC - Zechariah 11:12

"I told them, 'If you think it best, give me my pay; but if not, keep it." So they paid me THIRTY PIECES OF SILVER."

FULFILLED - Matthew 26:14-15

"Then one of the Twelve ~ the one called Judas Iscariot ~ went to

the chief priests and asked, 'What are you willing to give me if I hand him over to you?" So they counted out for him THIRTY SILVER COINS."

17. PROPHECY c. 485 BC - Zechariah 11:13
"And the Lord said to me, 'Throw it to the potter' ~ the handsome price at which they priced me! So I took the THIRTY PIECES OF SILVER AND THREW THEM INTO THE HOUSE OF THE LORD TO THE POTTER."

FULFILLED Matthew 27:5-7
"So Judas THREW THE MONEY INTO THE TEMPLE and left. Then he went away and hanged himself. The chief priests picked up the coins and said, 'It is against the law to put this into the treasury, since it is blood money.' So they decided to use the money to buy the POTTER'S field as a burial place for foreigners."

18. PROPHECY c. 485 BC - Zechariah 13:7
" 'Awake, O sword, against my shepherd, against the man who is close to me!' declares the Lord Almighty. 'Strike the shepherd, and the SHEEP WILL SCATTER.' "

FULFILLED - Matthew 26:31, 50, 56b
"Then Jesus told them, 'This very night you will all fall away on account of me, for it is written, 'I will strike the shepherd, and the sheep of the flock will be scattered'.... Then the men stepped forward, seized Jesus and arrested him....Then all the DISCIPLES DESERTED HIM AND FLED."

19. PROPHECY c. 700 BC - Isaiah 53:7
"He was oppressed and afflicted; yet he did not open his mouth; he was led like a lamb to the slaughter, and as a sheep before her shearers is silent, so he DID NOT OPEN HIS MOUTH."

FULFILLED - Matthew 27:12
" When he was accused by the chief priests and the elders, he GAVE NO ANSWER."

20. PROPHECY c. 1000 BC – Psalm 2:1-2

"Why do the nations conspire and the peoples plot in vain. The kings of the earth take their stand and the RULERS GATHER TOGETHER AGAINST his Anointed One."

FULFILLED - Luke 22:66; 23:1, 8

"At daybreak, the COUNCIL OF THE ELDERS of the people, both the chief priests and teachers of the law, met together and Jesus was led before them....then the whole assembly rose and led him off to [GOVERNOR] Pilate....When he learned that Jesus was under [KING] HEROD'S jurisdiction, he sent him to Herod who was also in Jerusalem at that time.

21. PROPHECY c. 1000 BC - Psalm 69:21

"They put GALL in my food, and gave me vinegar for my thirst."

FULFILLED - Matthew 27:34

"There they offered Jesus wine to drink, mixed with GALL; but after tasting it, he refused to drink it."

22. PROPHECY c. 1000 BC - Psalm 22:18

"*They DIVIDE MY GARMENTS among them and cast lots for my clothing.*"

FULFILLED - Matthew 27:35

"*When they had crucified him, they DIVIDED UP HIS CLOTHES by casting lots.*"

23. PROPHECY c. 700 BC – Isaiah 53:12

"He…made INTERCESSION for the transgressors."

FULFILLED - Luke 23:34

"Jesus said, 'Father, FORGIVE THEM, for they do not know what they are doing.' "

24. PROPHECY c. 1000 BC - Psalm 22:7-8

"*All who see me MOCK me; they hurl INSULTS, shaking their heads;* "*He trusts in the Lord; LET THE LORD RESCUE HIM. Let him deliver him, since he delights in him.*"

FULFILLED - Matthew 27:39, 41, 43

"*Those who passed by hurled INSULTS at him, shaking their*

head....In the same way the chief priests, the teachers of the law and the elders MOCKED him....'He trusts in God. LET GOD RESCUE HIM now if he wants him, for he said, "I am the Son of God." ' "

25. PROPHECY c. 700 BC - Isaiah 53:9
"He was assigned a GRAVE with the WICKED....
FULFILLED - Luke 23:32
"Two other men, both CRIMINALS, were also led out with him to be executed."

26. PROPHECY c. 1000 BC - Psalm 22:1
"MY GOD, MY GOD, WHY HAVE YOU FORSAKEN ME? Why are you so far from saving me, so far from the words of my groaning?"
FULFILLED - Matthew 27:46
"About the tenth hour Jesus cried out in a loud voice, 'Eloi, Eloi lama sabachthani?' ~ which means, 'MY GOD, MY GOD, WHY HAVE YOU FORSAKEN ME?'"

27. PROPHECY c. 1000 BC - Psalm 31:5
"INTO YOUR HANDS I COMMIT MY SPIRIT; redeem me, O Lord, the God of truth."
FULFILLED - Luke 23:46
"Jesus called out with a loud voice, 'Father, INTO YOUR HANDS I COMMIT MY SPIRIT.'"

28. PROPHECY c. 1000 BC - Psalm 34:20
"He protects all his BONES, NOT one of them will be BROKEN."
FULFILLED - John 19:32-33
"The soldiers therefore came and broke the legs of the first man who had been crucified with Jesus, and then those of the other. But when they came to Jesus and found that he was already dead, they did NOT BREAK HIS LEGS."

29. PROPHECY c. 485 BC - Zechariah 12:10
"And I will pour out on the house of David and the

inhabitants of Jerusalem a spirit of grace and supplication. They will look on me, the one they have PIERCED."
FULFILLED John 19:34
"Instead, one of the soldiers PIERCED JESUS' side with a spear, bringing a sudden flow of blood and water."

30. PROPHECY c. 700 BC - Isaiah 53:9
"He was...with the RICH IN HIS DEATH, though he had done no violence, nor was any deceit in his mouth."
FULFILLED Matthew 27:57-60
"As evening approached, there came a RICH MAN from Arimathea, named Joseph, who had himself become a disciple of Jesus. Going to Pilate, he asked for Jesus' body, and Pilate ordered that it be given to him. Joseph took the body, wrapped it in a clean linen cloth, and placed it in his OWN NEW TOMB that he had cut out of the rock."

31. PROPHECY c. 1000 BC - Psalm 45:6, 8
"Your throne, O God, will last for ever and ever; a scepter of justice will be the scepter of your kingdom....All your robes are fragrant with MYRRH AND ALOES and cassia."
FULFILLED - John 19:39
"He was accompanied by Nicodemus, the man who earlier had visited Jesus at night. Nicodemus brought a mixture of MYRRH AND ALOES, about seventy-five pounds. Taking Jesus' body, the two of them wrapped it with the spices, in strips of linen."

32. PROPHECY c. 700 BC - Hosea 6:2
"After two days he will revive us; on the THIRD DAY HE WILL RESTORE US, that we may live in his presence."
FULFILLED Matthew 27:62-64
"The next day, the one after Preparation Day, the chief priests and the Pharisees went to Pilate. 'Sir,' they said, 'we remember that while he was still alive that deceiver said, "After THREE DAYS I WILL RISE AGAIN."
John 19:42 - "Because it was the Jewish DAY OF PREPARATION and since the tomb was nearby, they laid Jesus there.

Luke 23:55-56 – "*...saw the tomb and how his body was laid in it. Then they went home...but they RESTED ON THE SABBATH ....*"

John 20:1,18 – *Early on the FIRST DAY OF THE WEEK [3]...Mary Magdalene went to the disciples with the news: 'I have seen the Lord!'* "

33. PROPHECY c. 1000 BC - Psalm 16:10-11

"Because you will NOT ABANDON ME TO THE GRAVE, nor will you let your Holy One see decay. You have made known to me the path of life; you will fill me with joy in your presence, with eternal pleasures at your right hand."

FULFILLED Matthew 28:5-6

"The angel said to the women, 'Do not be afraid, for I know that you are looking for Jesus who was CRUCIFIED. He is not here; he HAS RISEN just as he said.' "

35. What Does Jesus Dying On the Cross Have to do with Forgiveness?

**Forgiveness is not a simple thing
It has to do with God
taking Satan's power from him.**

What Things Are Sin?

Are you a sinner or a very good person to the point of being perfect? Actually, we cannot claim to be both. True, we may not murder, but let's look at the types of sin. There are three types:

1. Bad things we do
2. Bad things we think
3. Good things we do not do

The Bible and Quran probably pretty much list the same sins. The following comes from the scattered lists in the Bible (Romans 1:29-31; I Corinthians 6:9-1; Galatians 5:19-21; Ephesians 4:31, 541; Philippians 2:3,14; Colossians 3:8-9; I Timothy 1:9-10, 5:13, 6:35; II Timothy 3:2-8; Titus 3:3,9-11; James 3:14-16, 4:1-3, 5:3-6; I Peter 2:1, 4:3, II Peter 2:14-19; Jude 7:8,16; Revelation 21:8).

The easiest way to quickly look at them is in a chart. Here it is.

Bad We Do	Bad We Think	Good We Don't Do
Murder	Greed	Show gratitude
Adultery	Envy	Love good
Homosexuality	Deceit	Acknowledge truth
Gossip	Arrogance	Accept truth
Slander	Without faith	Pay wages
Boasting	Heartlessness	Support family
Prostitution	Hatred	Bear good fruit for God

Idolatry	Jealousy	Lend to someone in need
Stealing	Selfishness	Do good works in private
Drunkenness	Bitterness	Feed hungry
Swindling	Rage	Give thirsty a drink
Witchcraft	Anger	Visit people in prison
Fits of rage	Vanity	Devote self to others
Obscenities	Rebellion	Merciful
Coarse joking	Ungodliness	Contribute to others' needs
Foolish talk	Conceit	Hospitable
Complaining	Evil Suspicions	Do good to enemies
Arguing	Withholding truth	Obey the government
Lying	Loving money	Meet with God's people often
Filthy talk	Pride	Forgive
Law breaking	Without self-control	Gentle
Quarrelsomeness	Rashness	Pray without ceasing
Disobedience to parents	Weak willed	
Opposing truth	Coveting	
Enslaved to passions	Lusting	
Argumentative	Wrong motives	
Quarrelsome	Self-indulgent	
Divisive	Adulterous eyes	
Disorderly	Slavery to sin	
Hoarding wealth	Impatience	
Condemner of innocent	Cowardliness	
Hypocrisy	Vile	
Seducing	Vengeful	
Fault finder		
Grumbler		
Flatterer		
False healing		
Doing good for praise		
Sorcery		

From this list, we can see that everyone sins.

Here are three quick definitions of sin:

    1. Trespassing into hell
    2. Missing the target of heaven
    3. A fine, a debt.

Spiritual Laws That Cannot Be Broken

ABOUT GOD:

1. It is impossible for God to lie (Hebrews 6:18)
2. It is impossible for God to change (Malachi 3:6; Hebrews 13:8)
3. It is impossible for God to break a promise (Psalm 89:34)
4. It is impossible for God to be pleased with people without faith in him (Hebrews 11:6)
5. It is impossible for God to deny who he is (II Timothy 2:13)
6. It is impossible for God to sleep (Psalm 121:2-3)
7. It is impossible for God to judge wrong (Ecclesiastes 12:14)
8. It is impossible for God to be tempted to sin (James 1:13)

ABOUT SATAN:

1. It is impossible for Satan to tell the truth. He is the Father of Lies. (John 8:44)
2. It is impossible for Satan to give life. He is the originator of death (John 8:44)
3. It is impossible for Satan to do right. He is the originator of sin (Matthew 13:38)
4.. It is impossible for Satan to forgive. He is the accuser. (Revelation 12::10)
5. Satan always tempts people to sin (I Thessalonians 3:5)
6 He rules over everyone who sins (Ephesians 2:2)
7. He is the king of death (Hebrews 2:14)

WHERE DOES GOD LIVE? Heaven.
WHERE DOES SATAN LIVE? Hell

What Happens To Our Soul When We Sin?

1. We obey Satan (Hebrews 2:14)
2. We become separated from God (Isaiah 59:1-2)
3. We earn death (Romans 6:23)
4. The moment we sin, our soul dies (Genesis 2:17)

What Is Soul Death?

Technically, the word "death" means separation. When our body dies, we become separated from our body. When our body dies, we become separated from this earth. When our soul dies, we become separated from God who is Life (Job 33:4; Acts 17:25; John 1:3-4.

There is a "second death". "But the cowardly, the unbelieving, the vile, the murderers, the sexually immoral, those who practice magic arts, the idolaters and all liars--they will be consigned to the fiery lake of burning sulfur. This is the second death."

God cannot just forgive us. It is more complicated than that.

Every time we sin, our soul dies. Well, that is a terrible predicament to be in. But it is a spiritual law that cannot be broken.

Satan holds mankind hostage. Mankind is doomed to go to hell. Someone had to pay the ransom to get us out of hell (see Matthew 20:28 and Mark 10:45).

What is it that Satan wants? He wants his wages. His wages is death (Romans 6:23).

So, death is also the wage and is also the debt.

When we sin, we create a spiritual debt. We owe our souls to Satan. Our debt must be paid. It is a spiritual law that cannot be broken. This debt can also be called a fine. When we break the law, we are fined. Our government does not care who pays the debt as long as it is paid.

Have you ever gone into debt to the government—perhaps for taxes or a speeding fine--and borrowed the money from someone else to pay it? The government did not care who paid it, as long as the debt was paid.

Or, has anyone ever taken your punishment for you in other ways? Perhaps you were young and your parent insisted on a beating as punishment. Perhaps an older brother or sister who was bigger and stronger than you step in and say, "I did it. Punish me." The parent the one who admitted the guilt, then was satisfied and the wrong forgiven and forgotten.

Have you ever been threatened with reprimand within a company? If it was serious and you were a new employee, you expected to be fired over it? Perhaps someone who had been in the company a long time took the blame and did not lose his job? Then the matter was forgiven and dropped.

In all these cases, someone richer or stronger or more senior than you took the blame and took the punishment for you. Once the punishment had been meted out, the punisher was satisfied.

This is what Satan is like. He insists on the death punishment for our sin, and he does not care who pays the fine, the debt, the ransom, as long as it is paid.

You may say that is unfair. But, nothing Satan does is fair.

God Made It Possible for Us to Be Forgiven
By Entering Our World

If you owe a debt to a bank, then you pay the debt off, the bank issues a paper saying it has forgiven your debt.

How did God pay our debt of death to Satan (a spiritual

law that cannot be broken) so our debt could be forgiven? Remember, we live in a physical world. God on purpose put us in this physical world.

Then, God put a part of himself in the physical world. Injil (Gospel) John 1:1-3, 14 says "In the beginning [of the world] was the Word, and the Word was with God, and the Word was God. He was in the beginning with God. All things came into being through him, and apart from him nothing came into being that has come into being.... And the Word became flesh and dwelt among us, and we saw His glory, glory as of the only begotten from the Father, full of grace and truth"

How could Jesus be created and eternal both? Remember, Jesus was the Word of God placed in a human body. Words are spoken thoughts. Our thoughts have existed as long as we have, even though we create our thoughts.

Here are some other scriptures that state what John 1 said. The church of God was purchased with his own blood (Acts 20:28). God's glory was displayed in the face of Christ (II Corinthians 4:6). God said, "I will live with them and walk with them" (II Corinthians 6:16). Jesus existed in the form of God when he took on the likeness of men (Philippians 2:6). Jesus was the image of the invisible God, and all the fullness of God dwelled in him (Colossians 1:15-19). Jesus was the exact representation of God's nature (Hebrews 1:2). God was revealed in the flesh (I Timothy 3:16). Our great God and Savior was in Christ Jesus (Titus 2:11-13).

God in Jesus Paid our Debt/Ransom/Fine for Us Then Did What is Impossible for Us to Do

First, Jesus never sinned (Hebrews 4:15)

Second, he took the blame for every sin ever committed by mankind (II Corinthians 5:21; II Peter 2:24)

Third, he paid the ransom Satan demanded to free us from being his hostage and bound for hell (I Timothy 2:6)

AND Third, he paid the debt we owed to Satan (Romans 4:25; Isaiah 53:5)

On the cross that day, Jesus' body died. Also his soul died (Isaiah 53:11; Acts 2:31).

BUT HE CAME BACK TO LIFE. Jesus' soul immediately came back to life, and three days later, Jesus' soul re-entered that body.

Now that the fine had been paid, Satan became powerless to hold mankind hostage any longer. Remember, it is impossible for Satan to give life. Satan can only kill. God took over then, and brought the soul of mankind back to life. That is called FORGIVENESS – bringing our soul back to life.

But Not Everyone Is Forgiven

But, of course, that does not mean all of mankind will be able to go to heaven. We have to believe God did this for us. If we don't believe it, we cannot accept his ransom, and we still belong to Satan. We call this belief "faith". To demonstrate our faith to God, we imitate what that human body did for us: We die to our sinful nature, we are buried in a watery grave, then we come up out of our grave born again, our souls alive.

Then the rest of our life, we must continue to be loyal to God and try the best we can to do right. He will continue to forgive us, but only if we try not to sin. We cannot go around having all kinds of fun sinning because God will forgive us; it doesn't work like that. We must keep battling Satan our whole life because Satan wants us back. But if we keep returning to God, he will keep forgiving us. Then we are guaranteed heaven and do not have to wait until the Day of Judgment to know this.

36. Why Jesus Had to Die & Come Back To Life

Jesus said to her, "'I am the resurrection and the life. He who believes in me will live, even though he dies.'"
Injil, John 11:25

Death has been swallowed up in victory!
Where, O death, is your victory?
Where, O death, is your sting?
Thanks be to God! He gives us the victory through our Lord Jesus Christ!
Injil, 1st Corinthians 15:54b-57

ADAM, THE FIRST MAN ~ PHYSICAL & SINFUL

[Torah, Genesis 3:3, 19, 22]

God did say, 'You must not eat fruit from the tree that is in the middle of the garden, and you must not touch it, or you will DIE'"

To Adam God said, "Because you listened to your wife and ate fruit from the tree about which I

commanded you, 'You must not eat from it,' By the sweat of your brow you will eat your food until you return to the ground, since from it you were taken; for dust you are and to dust you will return [DIE]."

And the LORD God said, "The man has now become like one of us, knowing good and evil. He

must not be allowed to reach out his hand and take also from the tree of life and eat, and live forever."

MANKIND ~ PHYSICAL & SINFUL THROUGH ADAM

[Injil Romans 1:18, 21, 29-32]

The wrath of God is being revealed from heaven against all the godlessness and wickedness of people, who suppress the truth by their wickedness. For although they knew God, they neither glorified him as God, nor gave thanks to him, but their thinking became futile and their foolish hearts were darkened.

They have become filled with every kind of wickedness, evil, greed and depravity. They are full of envy, murder, strife, deceit and malice. They are gossips, slanderers, God-haters, insolent, arrogant and boastful; they invent ways of doing evil; they disobey their parents; they have no understanding, no fidelity, no love, no mercy. Although they know God's righteous decree that those who do such things DESERVE DEATH, they not only continue to do these very things but also approve of those who practice them.

[Romans 3:10-12, 23]

THERE IS NO ONE RIGHTEOUS, not even one; there is no one who understands; there is no one who seeks God. All have turned away, they have together become worthless; there is no one who does good, not even one. ALL HAVE SINNED AND FALL SHORT of the [sinless] glory of God,

ABRAHAM, FATHER OF FAITH, NOT WORKS

[Injil Romans 4:1-5, 16, 23-25]

What then shall we say that Abraham, our forefather

according to the flesh, discovered in this matter? IF, in fact, Abraham was justified by works, he had something to boast about—but not before God. What does Scripture say? "Abraham believed [had faith in] God, and it was credited to him as righteousness."

Now to the one who works, wages are not credited as a gift but as an obligation. However, to the one who does not work but trusts God who justifies the ungodly, their faith is credited as righteousness. Therefore, the promise comes by faith (not works), so that it may be by grace and may be guaranteed to all Abraham's offspring—not only to those who are of the law but also to those who have the faith of Abraham. He is the father of us all.

The words "it was credited to him" were written not for him alone, but also for us, to whom God will credit righteousness—for us who believe in him who raised Jesus our Lord from the dead. He was delivered over to death for our sins and was raised to life for our justification.

JESUS, THE SECOND ADAM ~ SPIRITUAL & SINLESS

[Injil Romans 5:6-8,12,14-15, 18-19, 21]

You see, at just the right time, when we were still powerless, Christ died for the ungodly. Very rarely will anyone die for a righteous person, though for a good person someone might possibly dare to die. But God demonstrates his own love for us in this: While we were still sinners, Christ died (physically and spiritually)
for us.

Therefore, just as sin entered the world through one man [Adam], and DEATH through SIN, and in this way death came to all people, because all sinned

Nevertheless, DEATH reigned from the time of Adam...even over those who did not sin by breaking a command, as did Adam, who is a pattern of the one to come.

But the GIFT is not like the trespass. For if the many died by the trespass of the one man [Adam], how much more did God's grace and the gift that came by the grace of the one man, Jesus Christ, overflow to the many!

Consequently, just as [Adam's] one trespass resulted in condemnation for all people, so also one righteous act resulted in justification and life for all people. For just as through the disobedience of the one man the many were made sinners, so also through the obedience of the one man [Jesus] the many will be made righteous.

So that, just as sin reigned in death, so also grace might reign through righteousness to bring eternal LIFE through Jesus Christ our Lord.

[Injil II Corinthians 5:20b-21; I Peter 2:21,22,24]

We implore you on Christ's behalf: Be reconciled to God. God made him [Jesus] who had no sin to be sin for us, so that in him we might become the righteousness of God.....To this you were called, because Christ suffered for you, leaving you an example, that you should follow in his steps. "He committed no sin, and no deceit was found in his mouth." "He himself [Jesus] bore our sins" in his body on the cross, so that we might die to sins and live for righteousness; "by his wounds you have been healed."

[Injil I Corinthians 15:20-22, 45,47-49]

But Christ has indeed been raised from the dead, the first fruits of those who have fallen asleep (died). For since DEATH came through a man [Adam], the resurrection of the dead comes also through a man. For as in Adam all DIE, so in Christ all will be made ALIVE.

So it is written: "The first man Adam became a living

being"; the last Adam, a LIFE-giving spirit. The first man was of the dust of the earth; the second man is of heaven. As was the earthly man, so are those who are of the earth; and as is the heavenly man, so also are those who are of heaven. And just as we have borne the image of the earthly man [Adam], so shall we bear the image of the heavenly man [Jesus].

MANKIND SPIRITUAL & SINLESS THROUGH JESUS:

[Injil Romans 6:3-11]

Or don't you know that all of us who were baptized into Christ Jesus were baptized into his DEATH? We were therefore buried with him through baptism into DEATH in order that, just as Christ was raised from the dead through the glory of the Father, we too may live a new LIFE.

For if we have been united with him in a DEATH like his, we will certainly also be united with him in a RESURRECTION like his. For we know that our old self was crucified with him so that the body ruled by sin might be done away with, that we should no longer be slaves to sin — because anyone who has died has been set FREE from sin.

The gospel God promised beforehand
through his prophets
in the Holy Scriptures
regarding his Son who,
as to his human nature was a descendant of David,
and who through the [Holy] Spirit of holiness
was declared with power [miraculously]
to be the Son of God
by his resurrection from the dead:

Jesus Christ our Lord.
Injil Romans 1:1b-4

Then death and Hades were thrown into the lake of fire;
the lake of fire is the second death.
Injil Revelation 20:14

GOD HAD TO BE MANIFEST IN A
HUMAN BODY
SO HE COULD DIE
AND COME BACK TO LIFE,
THUS CONQUERING DEATH FOR US

37. Did Jesus Die?

"And because of their saying: We slew the Messiah, Jesus
son of Mary, Allah's messenger –
they slew him not nor crucified him,
but it appeared so unto them;
and lo! those who disagree concerning it
are in doubt thereof;
they have no knowledge thereof save
pursuit of a conjecture;
they slew him not for certain".
Surah 4:157

Some Muslim scholars claim that Allah made Judas look like Jesus, and that is who was crucified.

Here is a contradictory statement from the Quran:

"(He) has made me (Jesus) kind to my mother, and not
overbearing or miserable;
So peace is on me the day I was born,
the day that I die."
Surah 19:32-33

PROOFS JESUS DIED

JESUS' APOSTLE JUDAS, IDENTIFIED HIM: Injil, Matthew 26:47-54 ~ While he was still speaking, Judas, one of the Twelve, arrived. With him was a large crowd armed with swords and clubs, sent from the chief priests and the elders of the people. Now the betrayer had arranged a signal with them: "The one I kiss is the man; arrest him." Going at once to Jesus, Judas said, "Greetings, Rabbi!" and kissed him. Jesus replied,
"Friend, do what you came for." Then the men stepped

forward, seized Jesus and arrested him. With that, one of Jesus' companions reached for his sword, drew it out and struck the servant of the high priest, cutting off his ear. "Put your sword back in its place," Jesus said to him, "for all who draw the sword will die by the sword. Do you think I cannot call on my Father, and he will at once put at my disposal more than twelve legions of angels? But how then would the Scriptures be fulfilled that say it must happen in this way?" [See also Injil, Mark 14:43-47; Luke 22:47-52; John 18:2-11]

THE POLICE HAD SEEN JESUS TEACHING OFTEN IN THE TEMPLE: Injil, Matthew 26:55 ~ At that time Jesus said to the crowd, "Am I leading a rebellion, that you have come out with swords and clubs to capture me? Every day I sat in the temple courts teaching, and you did not arrest me." [See also Injil Mark 14:48; Luke 22:53; John 18:12]

THE JEWISH RULERS HAD SEEN JESUS OFTEN IN THE TEMPLE: Injil, John 18:19-23 ~ "Meanwhile, the high priest questioned Jesus about his disciples and his teaching. "I have spoken openly to the world," Jesus replied. "I always taught in synagogues or at the temple, where all the Jews come together. I said nothing in secret. Why question me? Ask those who heard me. Surely they know what I said." When Jesus said this, one of the officials nearby struck him in the face. "Is this the way you answer the high priest?" he demanded. "If I said something wrong," Jesus replied, "testify as to what is wrong. But if I spoke the truth, why did you strike me?"

WITNESSES SAID HE WAS THE REAL JESUS BUT TAUGHT BAD THINGS: Injil, Matthew 26:59-62 ~ "Those who had arrested Jesus took him to Caiaphas, the high priest, where the teachers of the law and the elders had assembled. But Peter followed him at a distance, right up to the courtyard of the high priest. He entered and sat down with the guards to see the outcome. The chief priests and the whole Sanhedrin were looking for false evidence against Jesus so that they could put him to death. But they did not find any, though many false witnesses came forward. Finally, two came forward and declared, "This fellow said, 'I am able to destroy the temple of God and rebuild it in three days.' " Then the high priest stood up and said to Jesus, "Are you not going to answer? What is this testimony that these men are bringing against you?" [See also Injil, Mark 14:53-59]

PRINCE HEROD, THE GOVERNOR OF GALILEE WHERE JESUS GREW UP, SENT FOR JESUS TO PERFORM A MIRACLE: Injil, Luke 23:8-11 ~ "When Herod saw Jesus, he was greatly pleased, because for a long time he had been wanting to see him. From what he had heard about him, he hoped to see him perform some miracle. He plied him with many questions, but Jesus gave him no answer. The chief priests and the teachers of the law were standing there, vehemently accusing him. Then Herod and his soldiers ridiculed and mocked him. Dressing him in an elegant robe, they sent him back to Pilate."

PILATE WAS THE GOVERNOR IN JERUSALEM. HE EXECUTEDTHE MAN THEY ALL IDENTIFIED AS JESUS: Injil, Matthew 27:11-18,26 ~ "Meanwhile Jesus stood before the governor, and the governor asked him, "Are you the king of the Jews?" "Yes, it is as you say," Jesus replied. When he was accused by the chief priests and the elders, he gave no answer. Then Pilate asked him, "Don't you hear the testimony they are bringing against you?" But Jesus made no reply, not even to a single charge—to the great amazement of the governor. Now it was the governor's custom at the Feast to release a prisoner chosen by the crowd. At that time, they had a notorious prisoner, called Barabbas. So when the crowd had gathered, Pilate asked them, "Which one do you want me to release to you: Barabbas, or Jesus who is called Christ?" For he knew it was out of envy that they had handed Jesus over to him....He had Jesus flogged, and handed him over to be crucified." [See also Injil, Mark 15:1-15; Luke 23:1-7; 13-25; John 19:1-16]

THE JEWISH RULERS KILLED HIM FOR BLASPHEMY

~ **FOR CALLING HIMSELF THE SON OF GOD**: Injil, Matthew 26:63-66 ~ "But Jesus remained silent. The high priest said to him, "I charge you under oath by the living God: Tell us if you are the Christ, the Son of God." "Yes, it is as you say," Jesus replied. "But I say to all of you: In the future you will see the Son of Man sitting at the right hand of the Mighty One and coming on the clouds of heaven." Then the high priest tore his clothes and said, "He has spoken blasphemy! Why do we need any more witnesses? Look, now you have heard the blasphemy. What do you think?" "He is worthy of death," they answered. [See also Injil, Mark 14:60-64; Luke 22:66-71]

JUDAS HUNG HIMSELF AND, WHEN THE PRIESTS SAW WHO HE WAS, THEY USED HIS MONEY TO BURY HIM IN POTTER'S FIELD. EVERYONE IN JERUSALEM KNEW ABOUT IT: Injil Matthew 27:3-10; Acts 1:18-19 ~ When Judas, who had betrayed him, saw that Jesus was condemned, he was seized with remorse and returned the thirty pieces of silver to the chief priests and the elders. "I have sinned," he said, "for I have betrayed innocent blood." "What is that to us?" they replied. "That's your responsibility." So Judas threw the money into the temple and left. Then he went away and hanged himself. The chief priests picked up the coins and said, "It is against the law to put this into the treasury, since it is blood money." So they decided to use the money to buy the potter's field as a burial place for foreigners. That is why it has been called the Field of Blood to this day. Then what was spoken by Jeremiah the prophet was fulfilled: "They took the thirty pieces of silver, the price set on him by the people of Israel, and they used them to buy the potter's field, as the Lord commanded me."(With the payment he received for his wickedness, Judas [money] bought a field; there he fell headlong, his body burst open and all his intestines spilled out. Everyone in Jerusalem heard about this, so they called that field in their language Akeldama, that is, Field of Blood.)

38. What About Jesus' Throne Next to God?

The Quran states that Jesus did not die but God took him directly to heaven:

> "And because of their saying:
> We slew the Messiah, Jesus son of Mary, Allah's messenger –
> they slew him not nor crucified him,
> but it appeared so unto them;
> and lo! those who disagree concerning it
> are in doubt thereof;
> they have no knowledge thereof save
> pursuit of a conjecture;
> they slew him not for certain.
> No indeed, Allah raised him up to Him."
> Surah 4:157-158

Yes, God raised him up to heaven. Then what? The Bible says this:

> Who [is] he that is condemning?
> Christ [is] He that died,
> yea, rather also, was raised up;
> who is also on the right hand of God –
> who also doth intercede for us.
> Injil, Romans 8:34

If Christians believe Jesus died and went to heaven, is he sitting in a lesser throne next to God's greater throne? Does that prove Jesus was not God?

Not Two Thrones

There are not two thrones in heaven ~ one for God and one for Jesus with Jesus' throne sitting on the right side of God's throne.

In the Bible, any time there were two thrones, one at the right side of the king, the Bible says so. When King Solomon's mother came to the throne room, he always ordered her throne to be brought out and set at his right hand. (See Tanakh I Kings 2:19)

So, Where Is Jesus Sitting?

- At the right hand of Jehovah (Psalm 110:1)
- At my [God's] right hand (Matthew 22:44)
- At the right hand of the Mighty One (Matthew 26:64)
- At my [God's] right hand (Mark 12:36)
- At the right hand of the Mighty One (Mark 14:62)
- At the right hand of God (Mark 16:19)
- At my [God's] right hand (Luke 20:42)
- At the right hand of the Mighty One (Luke 22:69)
- To the right hand of God (Acts 2:33)
- At the my [God's] right hand (Acts 2:34)
- With his [God's] own right hand (Acts 5:31)
- At the right hand of God (Acts 7:55)
- At the right hand of God (Romans 8:34)
- At his [God's] right hand (Ephesians 1:20)
- At the right hand of God (Colossians 3:1)
- At the right hand of the Majesty in heaven (Hebrews 1:3)
- At my [God's] right hand (Hebrews 1:13)
- At the right hand of the throne of the Majesty (Hebrews 8:1)
- At the right hand of God (Hebrews 10:12)
- At the right hand of the throne of God (Hebrews 12:2)
- At God's right hand (I Peter 3:22)

The word "at" in the original Greek of the Injil New Testament is "en". This word is translated 114 times as "among", 129 times as "with", 302 times as "at", 1863 times as "ON". Therefore, using "ON the right hand of God" we have a whole new understanding and a whole new question.

What is the Right Hand of God?

- Created the world ~ 2 scriptures.
- Is his righteousness ~ 3 scriptures.
- Is his loving kindness ~ 2 scriptures.
- Cares for his people ~ 15 scriptures
- Conquers his people's enemies ~ 18 scriptures
- Is the Savior - 15 scriptures

Therefore, when Jesus came back to life and ascended to heaven, he took his place as our Savior who conquered our greatest enemies ~ Satan and Death.

Where is He in Relation to the Throne of God?

Remember, Jesus was the Word of God that we humans could see and hear physically. So, when he returned to heaven, he put off that physical shell but still as the Word of God (the Mind).

The Tanakh Bible explains it clearly.

"But about THE SON he says, YOUR THRONE, O God, will last for ever and ever" (Hebrews 1:8).

"I am the Living One; I was dead, and now look, I am alive for ever and ever....To the one who is victorious, I will give the right to sit with me on my throne, just as I was victorious and sat down WITH MY FATHER on his throne. (Revelation 1:18, 3:21).

"These in white robes...have washed their robes and made them white in the blood of the Lamb. Therefore, they are before the throne of God and serve him day and night in his temple; and he who sits on the throne will shelter them with his presence. 'Never again will they hunger; never again will they thirst. The sun will not beat down on them,' nor any scorching heat. For the LAMB [Jesus] AT THE CENTER OF THE THRONE will be their shepherd; 'he will lead them to springs of living water. And God will wipe away every tear from their eyes.' " (Revelation 7:13-17).

Jesus is not and never was an inferior God on a separate throne. He is God the Word and sits on God's throne.

39. Paul, the Anti-Christian Terrorist As Told By Paul Himself

He was born in Turkey to a successful family. So they were able to send him to the best schools for the best education down in Palestine. "I was advancing in my religion beyond many of my own age among my people and was extremely zealous for the traditions of my fathers," he explains. [1]

Due to his high intelligence and extreme religious zeal, he was able to work his way up until, as a very young man, he was chosen to be on the ruling council in his city. It was during that time that Christians began to infiltrate. Something had to be done about these apostates. Jihad was declared.

"I too was convinced that I ought to do all that was possible to oppose the divinity of Jesus. And that is just what I did."

His initial first-hand experience in killing Christians was when a Christian leader was stoned to death. He was proud to have been part of it.

He began to destroy the church. Going from house to house, he dragged off men and women and put them in prison.[2]

"On the authority of the chief imam, I put many of the Christians in prison, and when they were put to death, I cast my vote against them."

Still not satisfied with his part in putting down the malicious Christians, he explains, "Many a time I went from one town to another to have them punished, and I tried to force them to denounce their new apostasy and return to the true faith."

His hatred for Christians continued to fester and grow. "I was so obsessed with persecuting them that I even hunted them down in foreign cities," he recalls.[3] "I was a violent man," he readily admits.[4]

"I persecuted the followers of this Way to their death, arresting both men and women and throwing them into prison. I even obtained letters from the chief imams to their associates in Damascus, and went there to bring these people as prisoners.

"About noon as I came near Damascus, suddenly a bright light flashed around me. I fell to the ground and heard a Voice say to me, 'Paul! Paul! Why do you persecute me?'

Thrown off balance for a moment, he got control of himself and called back to the Voice to identify himself. "Who are you?" he demanded. He hoped he could flush out this trickster and haul him away to prison ~ and of course death for daring to imitate the one and only God, the ultimate of all blasphemies.

" 'I am Jesus whom you are persecuting!' he told me."

He was shocked. No, this could not be! He had always defended God against the people who dared make Jesus God. After all, God needs no partners. He'd always been taught that. God is one. His head reeled as he tried to grasp what was going on. Was this a trick, or could it possibly be the real thing?

Fighting his confusion and now visibly trembling, his knees gave way. He fell the ground. Then he looked up, straining to see what he could not see. "What shall I do, Lord?" he shouted into the light. The Voice told him to go on into Damascus and there he would be told what to do next.

When the light disappeared, he heard the soldiers who were with him ask, "What was that light? What was that sound?" But Paul could not see them. He was blind.

"Get me to Damascus! Hurry!" he declared, his arms outstretched, trying to touch someone familiar. "My companions led me by the hand into Damascus, because the brilliance of the light had blinded me" he explains.[5]

Once in Damascus, Paul went into seclusion. For three days he wrestled between what he had always been taught was true, and what the Voice had told him was true. Which was the lie?

His blindness: That was a sign. The Voice had to have been that of God. Or was it? How could it be? Didn't God realize that everything he had been doing was always in the name of God, the one and only God? Hadn't he been defending God all this time?

Refusing to eat, back and forth, back and forth he went. Sometimes praying, sometimes beating his fist on the floor, sometimes screaming uncontrollably with tears that everything was going wrong. Terribly wrong.

Too much to bear. What was right? What was wrong? What was truth? What was a lie? He needed another sign. He needed to know for sure if everything he had been doing for God had actually been against God. It couldn't have been. But, what if....

In the mean time, a Christian elsewhere in Damascus ~ one of Paul' would-be prisoners ~ heard the same Voice. The Voice told him to go to Paul. He objected. "I have heard many reports about this man and all the harm he has done to your holy people. And he has come here with authority from the chief imams to arrest all who call on your name." His objections did no good.

The Voice said "Go" and so the man went to Paul. "If I die, I die" he thought to himself.[6]

When Ananias arrived and saw Paul was blind, he did what Jesus had taught, "Love your enemies, do good to those who despitefully use you."[7] He went up to Paul and gently put his hands on him. The blind man jerked back at first, fearful of what would be happening to him next. He backed against the wall. Was it one of those Christians? Was it his turn to be imprisoned? Instead, the Christian spoke to him softly.

"Brother Paul, the Lord ~ Jesus, who appeared to you on the road as you were coming here ~ has sent me so that you may see again and be filled with the Holy Spirit."

Immediately, something like scales fell from his eyes, and he could see again. Paul had been given his other sign.

He looked at the Christian. He had questions. Could he expect the Christian to actually know the answers? The questions began to flow. What had he been doing? Why were things going wrong? Could the Christians he had imprisoned ever forgive him? Could God ever forgive him? What about Jesus? Lord Jesus! Lord Jesus? Was he really Lord after all? Had he really been God on earth after all?

Paul now recalls what Ananias explained to him. " 'The God of our ancestors has chosen you to know his will and to see the Righteous One, Jesus, and to hear words from his mouth. You will be his witness to all people of what you have seen and heard."

Change sides? Is that what he needed to do? Change sides? Identify with the apostates? Become an apostate?

He continues, recalling what Ananias told him to do. "And now what are you waiting for? Get up, be baptized and wash your sins away, calling on his name.' "[8]

Paul knew he had to do it. In his heart, mind and soul he knew. They went out to the river, walked out into the water, and Paul was baptized....

Now what? What could he possibly do after his baptism? All the Christians were afraid of him. He needed more time to sort things out.

"But when God, who set me apart from my mother's womb and called me by his grace, was pleased to reveal his Son in me so that I might preach him among all nationalities, my immediate response was not to consult any human being.

"I went into Arabia. I did not receive the gospel from any man; rather I received it by revelation from Jesus Christ."[9]

"Even though I was once a blasphemer and a persecutor and a violent man, I was shown mercy because I acted in ignorance and unbelief.

"The grace of our Lord was poured out on me abundantly, along with the faith and love that are in Christ Jesus. Here is a trustworthy saying that deserves full acceptance: Christ Jesus came into the world to save sinners — of whom I am the worst.

"But for that very reason I was shown mercy so that in me, the worst of sinners, Christ Jesus might display his immense patience as an example for those who would believe in him and receive eternal life.

"Now to the King eternal, immortal, invisible, the only God, be honor and glory for ever and ever. Amen."10]

---

[1] Galatians 1:14

[2] Acts 8:1-3
[3] Acts 26:9-11
[4] I Timothy 1:13
[5] Acts 22:6-11
[6] Acts 9:1-15
[7] Matthew 5:44
[8] Acts 9:17-19
[9] Galatians 1:16,17,12
[10] I Timothy 1:13-17

40. The Bible Was Not Corrupted In the 7th Century

WE FOUND WHERE THE QUR'AN CONFIRMED THE
BOOKS OF MOSES, THE GOSPEL, ETC.

WE FOUND WHERE PART OF THE BOOK HAD BEEN
KEPT SECRET,
AND SOMETIMES INTERPRETED WRONG.

BUT WE NEVER FOUND ACCUSATIONS THAT THE
BOOK (BIBLE) HAD BEEN
CORRUPTED IN WRITING BY THE TIME OF
MOHAMMED.

Ibn Azzim was the first Muslim to ever claim the Bible had been corrupted. He made this new claim in the year AD 1056, 400 years after the death of Muhammad, the prophet of Islam.

Surah 2:83, 85 ~ And remember We took a Covenant from the Children of Israel....Then is it only a part of the Book that ye believe in, and do ye reject the rest? but what is the reward for those among you who behave like this but disgrace in this life? and on the Day of Judgment they shall be consigned to the most grievous penalty. For Allah is not unmindful of what ye do.

Surah 2:86 ~ We gave Moses the Book and followed him up with a succession of apostles; We gave Jesus the son of Mary Clear (Signs) and strengthened him with the holy spirit. Is it that whenever there comes to you an apostle with what ye yourselves desire not, ye are puffed up with pride?

Surah 2:109 ~ Quite a number of the People of the Book

wish they could turn you back to infidelity after ye have believed, from selfish envy, after the Truth hath become Manifest unto them: But forgive and overlook, Till Allah accomplish His purpose; for Allah Hath power over all things.

Surah 3:3 ~ It is He Who sent down to thee (step by step), in truth, the Book, confirming what went before it; and He sent down the Law (of Moses) and the Gospel (of Jesus).

Surah 3:78 ~ There is among them a section who distort the Book with their tongues: (As they read) you would think it is a part of the Book, but it is no part of the Book.

Surah 3:84 ~ "We believe in Allah, and in what has been revealed to us and what was revealed to Abraham, Isma'il, Isaac, Jacob, and the Tribes, and in (the Books) given to Moses, Jesus, and the prophets, from their Lord: We make no distinction between one and another among them, and to Allah do we bow our will (in Islam)."

Surah 4:136 ~ O you who believe! Believe in...the scripture which He sent to those before (him). Any who denies Allah, His angels, His Books, His messengers and the Day of Judgment has gone far, far astray.

Surah 5:15 ~ O people of the Book! There hath come to you our Messenger, revealing to you much that ye used to hide in the Book, and passing over much (that is now unnecessary). There hath come to you from Allah a (new) light and a perspicuous Book

Surah 5:44 ~ It was We who revealed the law (to Moses): therein was guidance and light. By its standard have been judged the Jews, by the prophets who bowed (as in Islam) to Allah's will, by the rabbis and the doctors of law: for to them was entrusted the protection of Allah's Book, and they were witnesses thereto

Surah 5:47 ~ Let the People of the Gospel judge by what Allah has revealed therein.

Surah 5:48 ~ To you We sent the Scripture in truth, confirming the scripture that came before it, and guarding it in safety.

Surah 5:68 ~ Say: "O People of the Book! ye have no ground to stand upon unless ye stand fast by the Law, the Gospel, and all the revelation that has come to you from your Lord."

Surah 5:110 ~ Then will Allah say: "O Jesus the son of Mary! Recount My favour to thee and to thy mother. Behold! I strengthened thee with the Holy Spirit, so that thou didst speak to the people in childhood and in maturity. Behold! I taught thee the Book and Wisdom, the Law and the Gospel

Surah 6:85, 89 ~ And Zakariyya (Zachariah) and John, and Jesus and Elias: all in the ranks of the Righteous: And Ishmael and Elish and Jonah and Lut (Lot)....These were the men to whom We gave the Book, and authority, and prophethood: if these (their descendants) reject them, Behold! We shall entrust their charge to a new people who reject them not.

Surah 6:91 ~ "Who then sent down the Book which Moses brought? a light and guidance to man: But ye make it into (separate) sheets for show, while ye conceal much (of its contents).

Surah 6:114 ~ They know full well, to whom We have given the Book, that it hath been sent down from thy Lord in truth. Never be then of those who doubt. The Word of your Lord does find its fulfillment in truth and in justice: none can change His Words.

Surah 6:154-155 ~ Moreover, We gave Moses the Book,

completing (Our favour) to those who would do right, and explaining all things in detail, and a guide and a mercy, that they might believe in the meeting with their Lord. And this is a Book which We have revealed as a blessing: so follow it and be righteous, that ye may receive mercy.

Surah7:169-170 ~ They inherited the Book....As to those who hold fast by the Book and establish regular prayer, never shall We suffer the reward of the righteous to perish.

Surah 10:37 ~ This Qur'an is not such as can be produced by other than Allah. on the contrary it is a confirmation of (revelations) that went before it, and a fuller explanation of the Book - wherein there is no doubt - from the Lord of the worlds.

Surah 10:94 ~ If thou wert in doubt as to what We have revealed unto thee, then ask those who have been reading the Book from before thee: the Truth hath indeed come to thee from thy Lord: so be in no wise of those in doubt.

Surah 11:17 ~ A witness from Himself doth teach, as did the Book of Moses before it, a guide and a mercy? They believe therein.

Surah 13:36 ~ Those to whom We have given the Book rejoice at what hath been revealed unto thee.

Surah 18:27 ~ And recite (and teach) what has been revealed to thee of the Book of thy Lord: none can change His Words, and none wilt thou find as a refuge other than Him.

Surah 20:133 ~ They say: "Why does he not bring us a sign from his Lord?" Has not a Clear Sign come to them of all that was in the former Books of revelation?

Surah 29:46 ~ And dispute ye not with the People of the Book, except with means better (than mere disputation), unless it be with those of them who inflict wrong (and injury): but say, "We believe in the revelation which has come down to us and in that which came down to you.

Surah 32:23 ~ We did indeed aforetime give the Book to Moses: be not then in doubt of its reaching (thee).

Surah 45:16 ~ We did aforetime grant to the Children of Israel the Book the Power of Command, and Prophethood; We gave them, for Sustenance, things good and pure

Surah 46:12 ~ And before this, was the Book of Moses as a guide and a mercy: And this Book confirms (it) in the Arabic tongue.

SOMETIMES "THE BOOK" REFERS TO THE QUR'AN ITSELF

SOMETIMES THE QUR'AN HAD BEEN CHANGED TO "SOMETHING BETTER."

Surah 2:2 ~ This is the Book; in it is guidance sure, without doubt, to those who fear Allah.

Surah 2:78 ~ And there are among them illiterates, who know not the Book, but (see therein their own) desires, and they do nothing but conjecture.

Surah 2:79 ~ Then woe to those who write the Book with their own hands, and then say:" This is from Allah," to traffic with it for miserable price! Woe to them for what their hands do write, and for the gain they make thereby.

Surah 2:106 ~ None of Our revelations do We ABROGATE or cause to be forgotten, but We substitute something better or similar: Knowest thou not that Allah Hath power over all things?

Surah 3:23 ~ Hast thou not turned Thy vision to those who have been given a portion of the Book? They are invited to the Book of Allah, to settle their dispute

Surah 4:105 ~ We have sent down to thee the Book in truth, that thou mightest judge between men, as guided by Allah. so be not (used) as an advocate by those who betray their trust

Surah 5:15 ~ O people of the Book! There hath come to you our Messenger, revealing to you much that ye used to hide in the Book, and passing over much (that is now unnecessary). There hath come to you from Allah a (new) light and a perspicuous Book.

Surah 13:36-19 ~ Those to whom We have given the Book rejoice....Thus have We revealed it to be a judgment of authority in Arabic....Allah does BLOT OUT OR CONFIRM what He pleases: with Him is the Mother of the Book.

Surah 41:3 ~ Book, whereof the verses are explained in detail; a Qur'an in Arabic, for people who understand.

Surah 46:12 ~ And before this, was the Book of Moses as a guide and a mercy: And this Book confirms (it) in the Arabic tongue.

41. Proofs the Bible Was Never Corrupted

The first four books of the New Testament ~ Matthew, Mark, Luke, John ~ are eye-witness accounts of the life and teachings of Jesus, the Christ.

The fifth book of the New Testament is eye-witness accounts of the beginnings and early years of the church as led by the apostles of Jesus, the Christ. The rest of the New Testament is teachings of God as given to Jesus' apostles to write.

Although the originals written by the apostles personally no longer exist, below are a few of the numerous papyri that still exist of hand-written copies. Keep in mind that copyists who lived (for example) 50 years after the death of an apostle could (and likely did) have personally known the apostle.

Magdalen Papyrus (P-64) has been dated AD 50-60, some twenty years after the death of Jesus and during the lifetime of all of his Apostles. It shows scriptures from Matthew chapter 26, and is exactly as we have it today.

John Rylands Papyrus (P-52) dated at about AD 100-120, some 15 years after the death of Jesus' Apostle John. It is written on both sides with John 18:31-33 on one side and John 18:35-38 on the other side.

The Chester Beatty Papyri (P45) contains Acts of the Apostles. The Chester Beaty Papyri (P46) are dated between 100 and 150 AD. They contain most of Apostle Paul's inspired writings: The majority of Romans, Hebrews, 1 Corinthians, 2 Corinthians, Ephesians, Galatians, Philippians, Colossians; and two chapters of 1st Thessalonians. It is written in a handwriting which has only been found in first-century manuscripts. Written about ten to twenty years after the death of Jesus' Apostle John.

The Bodmer Papyrus (P-66) is dated about AD 150, some

50 years after the death of Jesus' Apostle John. The Bodmer Papyrus (P-75) covers most of the Gospel of Luke and much of the Gospel of John. It is dated around AD 175-190, about 75 years after the death of Jesus' Apostles, John.

The Chester Beatty Papyri (P47) are dated between 150-190 AD and cover the book of Revelation. Written about 75 years after the last Apostle's (John's) death

Within some sixty years of the death of the last apostle of Jesus ~ John ~ (according to ancient historian Eusebius), the ENTIRE NEW TESTAMENT had been assembled with the same 27 books we have today.

The Muratonian Canon that still exists and is dated around 170 AD, about 70 years after the death of the last apostle of Jesus, John, lists the same New Testament books that we use today. Here is a translation from the Greek to English:

....The third book of the gospel is that according to Luke. Luke the well know physician wrote it in his own name, according to the general belief after the ascension of Christ when Paul had associated him with himself as one zealous for correctness. One who took pains to find out the facts. It is true that he had not seen the Lord in the flesh. Yet having ascertained the facts he was able to being his narrative with the nativity of John.

The fourth book of the gospel is that of John's, one of the disciples. In response to the exhortation of his fellow disciples and bishops he said "Fast with me for three days then let us tell each other whatever shall be reveled to each one." The same night it was reveled to Andrew, who was one of the apostles, that it was John who should relate in his own name what they collectively remembered. Or that John was to relate in his own name, they all acting as correctors. And so to the faith of believers there is no discord even although different selections are given from the facts in the individual books of the gospels. Because in all of them under the one guiding spirit all the things relative to his nativity, passion, resurrection, conversation with his disciples, and his twofold advent, the first in humiliation rising form contempt which took place and the second in the glory of kingly power which is yet to come, have been declared. What marvel it is then if John induces so consistently in his epistles these several things saying in person "what we have seen with our eyes and heard with our ears and our hands have handled, those things we have written." For thus he professes to be not only an eye witness but also a hearer and a narrator of all the wonderful things of the Lord in their order.

Moreover the Acts of all the apostles are written in one book. Luke so comprised them for the most excellent Theophilus because of the individual events that took place in his presence. As he clearly shows by omitting the passion of Peter. As well as the departure of Paul, when Paul went from the city of Rome to Spain.

Now, the epistles of Paul, what they are and for what reason they were sent they themselves make clear to him who will understand.

First of all he wrote at length to the Corinthians to prohibit the system of heresy, then to the Galatians against circumcision.

And to the Romans on the order of scriptures intimating also that Christ is the chief matter in them. Each of which is necessary for us to discuss seeing that the blessed apostle Paul himself, following the example of his predecessor John, writes to no more that seven churches by name, in the following order: Corinthians, Ephesians, Philippians, Colossians, Thessalonians, and Romans. But he writes twice for the sake of correction to the Corinthians and to the Thessalonians.

That there is one church defused throughout the whole earth is shown. by this seven fold writing and John also in the Apocalypse. Even though he writes the seven churches, he speaks to all.

But he wrote out of affection and love one to Philemon, one to Titus, two to Timothy and these are held sacred in the honorable esteem of the church catholic, in the regulation of Ecclesiastical discipline.

There are over 5,300 known ancient Greek manuscript copies and parts of the New Testament in Greek that have survived until today. They cover every word in the New Testament that Christians use today.

For a detailed study, we recommend this comprehensive book:
How We Got the Bible, *3d ed.: Revised and Expanded, By: Dr. Neil R. Lightfoot.*

42. Love Letters From God to You

(Fill your name in the blanks provided)

[Jesus' own words to you] "Come to me, _____, you who are weary and burdened, and I will give you rest. Take my yoke upon you and learn from me, _____, for I am gentle and humble in heart, and you will find rest for your soul. For my yoke is easy and my burden is light." From Matthew 11:28-29

[Jesus' own words to you] "No one, including you _____, who has left home or brothers or sisters or mother or father or children or fields for me and the gospel will fail to receive a hundred times as much in this present age (homes, brothers, sisters, mothers, children and fields ~ and with them, persecution) and in the age to come, _____, eternal life." From Mark 10:29-30

[Jesus' own words to you] "Therefore, I tell you, _____, do not worry about your life, what you will eat; or about your body, what you will wear. Life is more than food, and the body more than clothes. Consider the ravens: They do not sow or reap, they have no storeroom or barn; yet God feeds them. And how much more valuable you are, _____, than the birds!" From Luke 12:22-24

[Jesus' own words to you] "For God so loved you, _____, that he gave his one and only Son, that if you believe in him, you shall not parish but have eternal life." From John 3:16

"Repent and be baptized, _____, in the name of Jesus Christ for the forgiveness of your sins. And you, _____, will receive the gift of the Holy Spirit." From Acts 2:38

"In all these things you, _____, are more than a conqueror through him who loved you. For I am convinced that neither death nor life, neither angels nor demons, neither the present nor the future, nor any powers, neither height nor depth, nor anything else in all creation will be able to separate you, _____, from the love of God that is in Christ Jesus your Lord." From Romans 8:37-39

"Grace and peace to you, _____, from God our Father and the Lord Jesus Christ, who gave himself for your sins, _____, to rescue you from the present evil age, according to the will of your God and Father, to whom be glory for ever and ever." From Galatians 1:3-5

"Grace and peace to you, _____, from God our Father and the Lord Jesus Christ. Praise be to the God and Father of our Lord Jesus Christ, who has blessed you in the heavenly realms with every spiritual blessing in Christ. For he chose you in him before the creation of the world to be holy and blameless in his sight. In love he predestined you to be adopted as his daughter through Jesus Christ, in accordance with his pleasure and will ~ to the praise of his glorious grace, which he has freely given you, _____, in the One he loves. In him you, _____, have redemption through his blood, the forgiveness of sins, in accordance with the riches of God's grace, that he lavished upon you, _____, with all wisdom and understanding." From Ephesians 1:2-10

"Therefore, my dear _____, as you have always obeyed ~ not only in my presence, but now much more in my absence ~ continue to work out your salvation with fear and trembling, for it is God who works in you, _____, to will and to act according to his good purpose. Do everything without complaining or arguing, so that you may become blameless and pure, a daughter of God without fault in a crooked and depraved generation, in which you, _____, shine like a star in the universe." From Philippians 2:12-15

"Therefore, _____, as God's chosen daughter, holy

and dearly loved, clothe yourself with compassion, kindness, humility, gentleness and patience. Bear with other people and forgive whatever grievances you may have against another. Forgive, _____, as the Lord forgave you. And over all these virtues put on love, which binds them all together in perfect unity. Let the peace of Christ rule in your heart, _____, since as members of one body you were called to peace. And be thankful. Let the word of Christ dwell in your richly, _____, as you teach and admonish one another with all wisdom, and as you sing psalms, hymns and spiritual songs with gratitude in your heart to God. And whatever you do, _____, whether in word or deed, do it all in the name of the Lord Jesus, giving thanks to God the Father through him." From Colossians 3:12-17

"But since you, _____, belong to the day, be self-controlled, putting on faith and love as a breastplate, and the hope of salvation as a helmet. For God did not appoint you to suffer wrath but to receive salvation through your Lord Jesus Christ. He died for you, _____, so that, whether awake or asleep, we may live together with him. Therefore, encourage one another and built each other up, just as in fact you, _____, are doing. We ought always to thank God for you, _____, and rightly so, because your faith is growing more and more, and the love you have for others is increasing. Therefore, among God's churches, we boast about your perseverance and faith, _____, in all the persecutions and trials you are enduring. All this is evidence that God's judgment is right, and as a result you, _____, will be counted worthy of the kingdom of God, for which you are suffering. God is just, _____: He will pay back trouble to those who trouble you, and give relief to you who are troubled and to us as well. This will happen when the Lord Jesus is revealed from heaven." From II Thessalonians 1:3-7

"But you, daughter of God, flee from all this, and pursue righteousness, godliness, faith, love, endurance and gentleness. Fight the good fight of the faith, _____. Take hold of the eternal life to which you were called, _____, when you made

Christianity or Islam ~ The Contrast

your good confession in the presence of many witnesses. In the sight of God who gives life to everything; and of Christ Jesus, who while testifying before Pontius Pilate, made the good confession, I charge you, _____, to keep this command without spot or blame until the appearing of your Lord Jesus Christ." From I Timothy 6:11-14

"So do not be ashamed, _____, to testify about your Lord, or ashamed of Paul his prisoner. But join with me in suffering for the gospel, by the power of God, who has saved us and called you, _____, to a holy life ~ not because of anything you have done, but because of his own purpose and grace. This grace was given you, _____, in Christ Jesus before the beginning of time." From II Timothy 1:8-9

"At one time you too, _____, were foolish, disobedient, deceived and enslaved by all kinds of passions and pleasures. You lived in malice and envy, being hated and hating one another. But when the kindness and love of God your Savior appeared, he saved you, not because of righteous things you had done, but because of his mercy. He saved you, _____, through the washing of birth of baptism and renewed by the Holy Spirit whom he poured out on you generously through Jesus Christ your Savior, so that, having been justified by his grace, you might become an heir, having the hope of eternal life." From Titus 3:3-7

"I always thank my God as I remember you, _____, in my prayers, because I hear about your faith in the Lord Jesus and your love for all the saints. I pray that you, _____, may be active in sharing your faith, so that you will have a full understanding of every good thing we you have in Christ. Your love has given me great joy and encouragement, because you, _____, have refreshed the hearts of the saints." From Philemon 1:1-7

"Therefore, since you, _____, have a great high priest

who has gone through the heavens, Jesus the Son of God, hold firmly to the faith you profess. For you do not have a high priest who is unable to sympathize with your weaknesses, _____, but you have one who has been tempted in every way, just as you are ~ yet was without sin. Then approach the throne of grace with confidence, so that you may receive mercy and find grace to help you, _____, in your time of need." From Hebrews 4:14-16

"Consider it pure joy, _____, whenever you face trials of many kinds, because you know that the testing of your faith develops perseverance. Perseverance must finish its work so that you, _____, may be mature and complete; not lacking in anything. If you lack wisdom, _____, you should ask God who gives generously to all without finding fault, and it will be given to you." From James 1:2-5

"Praise be to the God and Father of your Lord Jesus Christ. In his great mercy, he has given you new birth, _____, into a living hope through the resurrection of Jesus Christ from the dead, and into an inheritance that can never perish, spoil or fade ~ kept in heaven for you, _____, who through faith are shielded by God's power until the coming of the salvation that is ready to be revealed in the last time. In this you greatly rejoice, though now for a little while you, _____, may have had to suffer grief in all kinds of trials. These have come so that your faith, _____ ~ of greater worth than gold, which perishes even though refined by fire ~ may be proved genuine and may result in praise, glory, and honor when Jesus Christ is revealed. Though you, _____, have not seen him, you love him; and even though you do not see him now, you believe in him and are filled with an inexpressible and glorious joy, for you, _____, are receiving the goal of your faith, the salvation of your soul." From I Peter 1:3-9

"For this very reason, _____, make every effort to add to your faith goodness; and to goodness, knowledge; and to knowledge, self-control; and to self-control, perseverance; and to perseverance, godliness; and to godliness, sisterly kindness; and to sisterly kindness, love. For if you possess these qualities in increasing measure, they will keep you, _____, from being ineffective and unproductive in your knowledge of our Lord Jesus Christ." From II Peter 1:5-8

"How great is the love the Father has lavished on you, _____, that you should be called a daughter of God! And that is what we are! The reason the world does not know us is that it did not know him. Dear _____, now we are children of God, and what we will be has not yet been made known. But we know that when he appears, we shall be like him, for we shall see him as he is. You who have this hope in him, _____, purifies yourself, just as he is pure." From I John 3:1-3

"Watch out that you do not lose what you have worked for, _____, but that you may be rewarded fully. If you run ahead and do not continue in the teaching of Christ, you do not have God; if you continue in the teachings, _____, you have both the Father and the Son." From II John 8-9

"Peace to you, _____." From III John 14

"To him who is able to keep you, _____, from falling and to present you before his glorious presence without fault and with great joy." From Jude 24

"Never again will you hunger, _____, never again will you thirst. The sun will not beat upon you, nor any scorching heat. For the Lamb at the center of the throne will be your shepherd, _____; he will lead you to springs of living water. And God will wipe away every tear from your eyes, _____." From Revelation 7:16-17

43. Gear for the Christian Soldier

Finally, be strong in the Lord and in his mighty power.
Put on the full armor of God,
so that you can take your stand
against the devil's schemes.

For our struggle is not against flesh and blood,
but against the rulers,
against the authorities,
against the powers of this dark world
and against the spiritual forces of evil
in the heavenly realms.

Therefore put on the full armor of God,
so that when the day of evil comes,
you may be able to stand your ground,
and after you have done everything,
to stand.

Stand firm then,
with the belt of truth buckled around your waist,
with the breastplate of righteousness in place,
and with your feet fitted with the readiness
that comes from the gospel of peace.

In addition to all this,
take up the shield of faith,
with which you can extinguish all the
flaming arrows of the evil one.

Take the helmet of salvation
and the sword of the Spirit,

which is the word of God.

And pray in the Spirit on all occasions
with all kinds of prayers and requests.

Peace to the brothers and sisters,
and love with faith from
God the Father and the Lord Jesus Christ.
Grace to all who love our Lord Jesus Christ
with an undying love.

{Injil Ephesians 6:10-18, 23-24}

44. Words of Courage

As a result, it has become clear throughout the whole palace guard and to everyone else that I am in chains for Christ. 14 And because of my chains, most of the brothers and sisters have become confident in the Lord and dare all the more to proclaim the gospel without fear....Yes, and I will continue to rejoice, 19 for I know that through your prayers and God's provision of the Spirit of Jesus Christ what has happened to me will turn out for my deliverance. 20 I eagerly expect and hope that I will in no way be ashamed, but will have sufficient courage so that now as always Christ will be exalted in my body, whether by life or by death. 21 For to me, to live is Christ and to die is gain. (Philippians 1:13-14, 18-21)

"Do not be afraid of those who kill the body but cannot kill the soul. Rather, be afraid of the One who can destroy both soul and body in hell. 29 Are not two sparrows sold for a penny? Yet not one of them will fall to the ground outside your Father's care. 30 And even the very hairs of your head are all numbered. 31 So don't be afraid; you are worth more than many sparrows. 32 "Whoever acknowledges me before others, I will also acknowledge before my Father in heaven." (Jesus, Matthew 10:28-32)

So do not be ashamed of the testimony about our Lord or of me his prisoner. Rather, join with me in suffering for the gospel, by the power of God. 10 It has now been revealed through the appearing of our Savior, Christ Jesus, who has destroyed death and has brought life and immortality to light through the gospel. (II Timothy 1:8-10)

Always be prepared to give an answer to everyone who asks you to give the reason for the hope that you have. But do this with gentleness and respect, 16 keeping a clear conscience, so that those who speak maliciously against your good behavior in Christ may be ashamed of their slander. (I Peter 3:15-16)

Do not be anxious about anything, but in every situation, by prayer and petition, with thanksgiving, present your requests to God. 7 And the peace of God, which transcends all understanding, will guard your hearts and your minds in Christ Jesus.(Philippians 4:6-7)

Then they called them again and commanded them not to speak or teach at all in the name of Jesus. But Peter and John replied, "Which is right in God's eyes: to obey you rather than God? You be the judges! (Acts 4:18-19)

Therefore, among God's churches we boast about your perseverance and faith in all the persecutions and trials you are enduring. 5As a result you will be counted worthy of the kingdom of God, for which you are suffering. 16 Now may the Lord of peace himself give you peace at all times and in every way. The Lord be with all of you. (II Thessalonians 1:4-5, 3:16)

45. Some Christian Poetry

Jesus, Thou joy of loving hearts,
Thou Fount of life, Thou Light of men,
From the best bliss that earth imparts,
We turn unfilled to Thee again.

Thy truth unchanged hath ever stood;
Thou savest those that on Thee call;
To them that seek Thee, Thou art good,
To them that find Thee, all in all!

Bernard of Clairvaux
About 1120

Jesus Christ is risen today, Al-le-lu-ia!
Our triumphant holy day, Al-le-lu-ia!
Who did once upon the cross, Al-le-lu-ia!
Suffer to redeem our loss, Al-le-lu-ia!

Unknown Christian
About 1350

A mighty fortress is our God, a Bulwark never failing;
Our helper He, amid the flood of mortal ills prevailing.
For still our ancient foe doth seek to work us woe;
His craft and power are great, and armed with cruel hate,
On earth is not his equal.

And tho this world, with evil filled, Should threaten to undo us;
We will not fear, God hath willed His truth to triumph thru us.
Let goods and kindred go, this mortal life also;

Christianity or Islam ~ The Contrast

The body they may kill: God's truth abideth still,
His kingdom is forever!

Martin Luther
About 1530

Fairest Lord Jesus! Ruler of all nature!
O Thou of God and man the Son!
Thee will I cherish, Thee will I honor,
Thou my soul's glory, joy, and crown.

Unknown Christian
1677

Must Jesus bear the cross alone,
And all the world go free?
No, there's a cross for everyone,
And there's a cross for me.

The consecrated cross I'll bear
Till he shall set me free,
And then go home my crown to wear,
For there's a crown for me.

Thomas Shepherd
1693

And can it be that I should gain
An interest in the Savior's blood?
Died He for me, who caused His pain?
For me, who Him to death pursued?
Amazing love! How can it be
That Thou, my God, shouldst die for me?

Charles Wesley
1738

46. Organization of the Bible

The Bible is actually 66 small books assembled together into one large volume. It has two divisions ~ the Old Testament written for the Jews, and the New Testament written for the Christians. Christians do read the Old Testament however because it contains so many prophecies about Jesus Christ.

DIVISIONS OF THE OLD TESTAMENT
Written for Jews

BOOKS OF LAW & HISTORY
Covers about 4000 ~ 1400 BC
5 Books: Genesis, Exodus, Leviticus, Numbers, Deuteronomy
They begin with the creation of the world and progress to the creation of the Jewish nation. They also itemize the Law of Moses which consists of some 600 commandments, not just the Ten Commandments people hear so much about.

BOOKS OF HISTORY
Covers about 1400 ~ 450 BC
12 Books: Joshua, Judges, Ruth, 1st & 2nd Samuel, 1st & 2nd Kings, 1st & 2nd Chronicles, Ezra, Nehemiah, Esther
They cover establishment of the Jewish nation, its downfall, and its eventual but weak return to power In the Promised Land.

BOOKS OF POETRY
Covers about 300 ~ 1000 BC
5 Books: Job, Psalms, Proverbs, Ecclesiastes, Song of Songs (sometimes called Song of Solomon)
Job took place during the time of Genesis, while the other

four were written during the time of II Samuel and I Kings.

MAJOR PROPHETS
Covers about 700 ~ 530 BC
5 Books: Isaiah, Jeremiah, Lamentations, Ezekiel, Daniel.

Most of these prophets lived during the downfall of the Jewish nation as told in II Kings and II Chronicles. Some lived when the Jews returned to their Promised Land from exile in Babylon/Persia (Iran & Iraq), and restored it nearly a century later. They all prophesied a coming divine Messiah who would set up an eternal kingdom of heaven and save the world from our sins.

MINOR PROPHETS
Covers about 750 ~ 430 BC
12 Books: Hosea, Joel, Amos, Obadiah, Jonah, Micah, Nahum, Habakkuk, Zephaniah, Haggai, Zechariah, Malachi.

These prophets were not less important than the major prophets; they just wrote much shorter books. They, too, lived during the accounts of I & II Kings and I & II Chronicles. They, too, all prophesied a coming divine Messiah who would set up an eternal kingdom of heaven and save the world from our sins.

DIVISIONS OF THE NEW TESTAMENT
Written for Christians

LIFE OF CHRIST
Covers about 1 AD - 33 AD
4 Books: Matthew, Mark, Luke, John.

Each author ~ two were apostles ~ gives his own memories of Jesus' birth, ministry, death, resurrection and ascension to heaven from different points of view, and fulfillment of centuries-old prophecies of Jesus as the eternal Messiah.

BOOK OF HISTORY

Covers about 33 AD - 65 AD
One Book: Acts of the Apostles

Beginning with the ascension of Jesus to heaven, it progresses through the establishment of the church (the Kingdom of Heaven on earth) over a period of 30 years, and how people became Christians under the direction of the Apostles.

BOOKS ON CHRISTIAN LIFE BY APOSTLE PAUL

Covers about AD 50 – about AD 68

13 Books: Romans, I & II Corinthians, Galatians, Ephesians, Philippians, Colossians, I & II Thessalonians, I & II Timothy, Titus, Philemon,

It's easy to become a Christian. The hard part is living the Christian life afterwards. That's what these books are all about.

BOOKS ON CHRISTIAN LIFE BY APOSTLES JAMES, PETER, JOHN & JUDE

Covers about AD 68 - 90

8 Books - Hebrews, James, I & II Peter, I , II & III John, Jude.

Again, it's easy to become a Christian. The hard part is living the Christian life afterwards. And so the other apostles wrote encouragement too. All writers were inspired by God what to say.

BOOK OF PROPHECY

Covers about 95 AD

1 Book: Revelation

This book was written to Christians being threatened with torture and execution for believing Jesus is the Son of God. Its theme is "God Keeps His Promises and Will Take Care of You." Some applies to the past, some to the present, some to the future. This symbolic book can be interpreted through the numerous Old Testament events to which it refers.

47. Testimonies of 100 Muslims Who Decided Jesus Really Was the Son of God Not Just a Prophet

Spelling left as written. Countries they live in taken out for their safety.

Semi-Professional in Middle East in 40s: I like to read the Bible. Please send me one secretly. The prophecies of Jesus in Isaiah are very meaningful to me. I want to make a decision to be Christian but now it is very dangerous for me. I and wife have been baptized in secret. Tell me how to pray to the Christian God.

Professional in Europe in 20s: Can you send me Bible? I'm Muslim but I and my friends decided to turn in to Christianity. I wonder about God's work and started to read Bible.

Semi-Professional in Middle East in 20s: I am very impressed with this story and very sad for Jesus. I wish I can return in time and be beside him. I learned to love Jesus. Jesus is the truth and no one can deny this. Lifting him from death was truth and not imagination. Jesus is truth and peace from the beginning until the end of the world. Jesus lifted from death to be on the right side of God.

Professional in Middle East in 30s: I don't have any experience with BIBLE with a Muslim background
....I know that Jesus came to fulfill the Old Testament and have a perfect life but honestly I did not know that there are such details related between Jesus and the plan of God.... I am so glad I did it with the right way because I do not want to reject God's purpose. I am proud that I changed my whole belief about Christ

and became Christian even though that was against everybody I know and I became threatened to die for my belief but I know even if I die that will be the door for my eternal life through faith in Jesus Christ.

Professional in Middle East in 60s: Jesus Christ the Son of God is the Lord and Savior. God revealed himself to people through his Son. Jesus had the power and heart of God, and had the power on earth to forgive sins.

Professional in Middle East in 50s: I believe and I agree that the earth and sky was begun by God, and it can be ended by God. I believe in the Muslim Surahs... I learned that Jews do not believe in every thing the Old Testament says.... Jesus is prophet and savior, even I as a Muslim is ordered by Allah to believe in Jesus Miracles by the power of God.... I learnt that God makes repentance for all people and that because Jesus sacrificed for sake of all people... I hope you understand my position I started to feel that I am very close to what you have taught me, no body forces me to be satisfied with any thing but that I am satisfied. I am ready to meet any Christian you send to me.

Semi-Professional in Middle East in 20s: This is the first time I saw the Quran in the English language. I was Shocked! I want to know more about Jesus Christ.

Semi-Professional in Middle East in 30s: Many times recently I felt very devastated because of my situation. But when I look to the daily scripture, I see myself there and it refreshes my faith. At the beginning I asked my self why everything collapsed in my life when I became Christian. But from the Bible I knew the answer. The reason is not because I am weak, but because I am a new fighter for God. And I became so strong in Satan's eyes and he became so terrified that he tried to do his best to discourage me. So I smiled and told him do his best .... ultimately I will win because I have God with me.

Semi-Professional in Europe in 30s: I lived with the Muslim religion all my life, but as I got older, I was not convinced it was right. Several years ago I got a Bible and read many Bible scriptures without the help of anyone. I was very touched by the history of Jesus, his life and his death. When I read the details of the crucifixion, I wept. In 2001, I met some Christians who explained things in the scriptures on salvation, and all that I had read before was more clear. I was baptized and now live in _____. I am faithful in the Church of Christ.

Semi-Professional in Middle East in 40s: The next king will be descendant of David and will be called "the Son of God."....2010 years people still remembering His name worshiping Him....There was a change in Jesus, that is part of supernatural.... He died for people, He lived for people. His life end and remembering all over the world still now.

Professional in Middle East in 20s: I didn't really know the real idea behind baptism. I knew that baptism with water like washing sins from people. And to be honest with you, I thought that this is meaningless. However, when I learned about changing souls and lives, get close to God and Jesus and be really alive with God's mercy, this ideas make things more clear and meaningful.

Semi-Professional in Africa in 50s: Jesus' rising was the greatest event in the history of world. Baptism is very important for anybody to be real Christan. Baptism's vital is coming from the New Birth

Laborer in Middle East in 30s: When we look at Jesus, we see what God is like".... Jesus have power over sickness and disease. Jesus can forgive sins, and only truly God can forgive sins. So, Jesus shows us the proof that he is son of God.... Anyone who is not born of water and the Spirit cannot enter God's kingdom"

Professional in Middle East in 40s: (Jesus didn't die

because the Lord protect him from Satan followers
….Baptize is so important to complete that agreement for forgiveness . Bad things will stop and give us moral and spiritual power by living Holy Spirit in our bodies….He know must wash himself by water to remove sins from his body… the Bible isn't tale book….Bible is trustworthy…..That is prove the Bible is God's word….The Bible still trustworthy regardless. All skeptics are thinking in different ways but finally will find the right direction because these words of God….We feel guilty and need to back on the right track to God. the penalty paid by Jesus for our sins….The Bible is lighting the road front of us to can't see the truth and wash our sins away by follow the Christ to get rest in your life. …His son came to save us to eternal life. So, Jesus defeated Satan….. His son so pleased by God…..Baptism repesented stages of Christ that he passed ,Like death, burial and resurrection….If you want to born again you have to baptism to begin new life… we want and let our old sinful die with Christ on the cross…. Holy Spirit and God help me and provides away of escape.

Professional in Middle East in 20s: I want to send me all Book about Bible, Please . I want to have these Book. And you knew these Books [of Bible] is not sales in my country because this is a Islamic Country and Unfortunately those Books is forbidden and have penalty if anyone sales open. If you have this Books [of Bible] please send me in my Email i want to read all books in my phone. of coures i have to hide these books far of the other families man and woman because its dangerous for me.

Professional in Middle East in 40s: The most sadness fills my heart with pain. It was a horrible, blood scene [crucifixion]….Jesus appeared to tell them he was alive again….

Professional in Middle East in 40s: l learned many things about Isaiah, The prophet the new king I did not know before that…. I learned new things about Jesus like The word "Messiah"…. I learned some informations about Jesus as a son of

God and how the earthquake happened when he was died.... those who seek God and find him in Jesus Christ.... Baptism is a symbol of the death, that we share Jesus with his death , burial our sins body in water, and resurrection when we return back to life.... The word "baptism" means "immersion in water as a holy thing ..... the important of baptism that let us forgivness from god for our sins.

Housewife, in Middle East in 50s: A prophet who will have God's Spirit in him and will suffer a lot to take our sins away and will be fully human and fully God....God put his Holy Spirit in Mary to bring the savior....God's son can forgive sins. Yes, I believe that Jesus truly was the son of God because
God had put his soul in him....Some Muslims believe God chose Jesus to be his son spiritually and I have to admit they are few

Professional in Middle East in 30s: ....understand more than I imagined....Jesus sacrificed himself to erase people's sins....I did not baptize. I do not know even how to do that. Would you tell me?...When I am immersed in water, my previous sins will be erased....new life like a baby that never sinned.

Semi-Professional in Middle East in 20s Jesus was the Son of God. The Bible is the Book of God, Word of God. It's never late to start life again.

Professional in Europe in 20s: I believe more in God....Jesus is the Messenger of God as their savior....God sent Jesus to help people choose the right way and do away from sin....Jesus was king of God because he was the son of God....Jesus is the son of God. ...Jesus gives life....accepting the resurrection of Jesus....God is able to achieve our resurrection after death and I am very confident in the strength of this
....being baptized he will be cleansed from sins....baptism is the method of purification of the soul and reach God....Jesus

was pure, without sin...Jesus is the Son of God....Baptism symbolizes purification of sin and the launch of a road without sin and closer to God....Baptism is an important thing to be done in life and it pleases God.

Retired, in Middle East in 60s: Prediction that a descendant of Eve, whose name is the Son of God...kill Satan...true king....the Spirit of the Lord on earth....incarnation of God's Spirit and took his image to live among ordinary people....sent from God to give his life for others....Jesus claimed to be the Son of God...set people free...and forgive...sinful. Jesus demonstrated his divine power...as a dove to rest on Jesus, the voice of God shouted "This is my Son!"....Jesus was a servant king....hailed by a voice coming from a bright cloud....Jesus really the son of God...raised from death....I need to read and learn more.

Laborer in United States in 30s: .... the New Kingdom what His message will be to the People, when is He coming, And where He will be announce .... I have learned HOW much Jesus loves us,How He raised from death And how much He sacrificed His life for US.... He has the power to forgive sin,... when we look at Jesus we see what God is look like.... I do go to the church some times on Sunday with my friends.... the bible is word of God, if you look at the history of the bible.... there is NO doubt its word of God....I was born as Muslim I grew up in muslim family I have read the Quran but honestly most Muslim including my self they read the Quran but they don't understand it. Lock of explanation lead to a big problem to most Muslim. you have to go to Islamic university....so you can learn and understand the explanation of Quran....after I read the Quran I ASKED too many people to explain to Me the different between Islam and Christianity all the answer I got the same answer they only believe Islam is the right religion. When I ask people that who are well educated for an explanation they said they don't want to go so far according to the religion.

Semi-Professional in Middle East in 30s: at last I have

learned that a descendent of David will be the next king and he Is called "the son of God" , and like David he will be a Shepherd - King....

Professional in Middle East in 60s: ....Mary and her family and the story of the Son of the God

Professional in Middle East in 30s: That descendant (in the flesh) was Jesus with God's Spirit in him. So, being born again referred to baptism in water. When we come up out of the water, we are born again spiritually, our souls come alive forever....Jesus the king came to of the world for people to know the truth, and erase their sins.... Jesus] Defeat of Satan...The baptism is very important to purify us from the sins ...Christ came to cleanse us from our sins and died for us....The Bible is the Word of God.

Semi-Professional in Middle East in 40s: God the all mighty know every thing from the biginning to the end of the world, and he sent Jesus for us to save us from sins and show us the right path..... I BELIVE IN ONE God. Jesus Christ is the Spirit of God.... Jesus was like God are the power of return from the death to life...

Professional in Middle East in 50s: We are waiting to the Son of God to save us from evil....I am always remember the saying of Jesus Christ "Father, forgive these people.... Jesus born and died to sacrifice or us.... Really , I like this sentence "Other religions want you to die for their leader, but their leader does not die for them."....

Professional in Middle East in 30s: Jesus is the true king and more than a man....Jesus really had been raised from death, and this is not a fable....God's plan that Jesus was born in Bethlehem, died by a cross, then...raised from death....We must go back to Bible so we know truth.

Laborer in Middle East in 20s: This is very good information...I try to buy these books [of the Bible]....but Islamic boy killed his Christian teacher here....Mary was pregnant of the Holy Soul....the Baby was God's Son. When God's Holy Spirit enters someone, he is God's son....I am shocked about Jesus' amazing proofs [prophecies fulfilled]....Jesus rising from death is evidence to show all hypocrites that Jesus is the only son of God. I felt my soul fly to heaven....Quran doesn't let us ask any opposite questions....I wished to have a Christian friend but that never happened; and now when I know you and about Christians, I love them more......Please pray for me, but I couldn't be baptized because my family won't let me. I am afraid too much. I have a plan to do that one day....in which nobody break off relations with me....I thank you till the moment of my grave....I am afraid of reactions...now I am very worried....In Islam they don't accept any opposite idea; if you don't believe them, they kill you....I am afraid....I did it. I baptized. I am free!

Unemployed in Middle East in 20s: I have learned the Isaiah's his vision of the spiritual kingdom , the new king and the king would be a suffuring servant .... I have learned that the king was suffering - Jesus promised his followers a home in heaven - his arrest - his judgement by Pilate- his dies on the cross and his kingdom.

Professional in Middle East in 50s: Jesus was not a man like any other man, he was superior; he was divine.

Professional in Far East in 60s: For the first time I learned that a bad person can be chosen by God for future work.... now I understood that God always has good plans for me.... The relationship between God and man was destroyed by sin, but God restored it. Jesus took the punishment of all the human being without uttering a word....

Professional in Canada in 30s: Scientific discovery is just a fact mentioned by the Bible 2000 years ago and this is the scientific miracles of the Bible....God will save from the sin by sending the Savior as a Sacrifice for the human beings.... to be honest this is our first time to read Bible and we like it so much.... think about the Bible and Jesus....Jesus sent from God to defeat Sin and Satan. The Bible is the Word of God....the church is the most important way to follow the Word of God....Jesus is the king of the Kingdom of God and the Word of God....Jesus really had been raised from death....God sent Jesus to erase our sins and defeat Satan

Semi-Professional in Africa in 20s: God sent Jesus to the people to save from the sin.

Professional in Middle East in 30s: Jesus said rivers of life flow out from his heart. He was talking about a Holy Spirit....he was more than a man....To be free from sin, God even sent his Son to suffer and bless us....God is great to send his son, Jesus, to defeat Satan....He could protect his Son, but for us it happened....To be baptized to share Jesus raised from death and run away from sins, so we will have the Holy Spirit in our bodies....The church is everywhere and spread among the world that interpret the prophecy's word more than 2000 years before....Jesus went back to his Father to sit in his right place with all authority given him, but his spirit still was with his apostles....We need to follow the great Son who is Jesus....They can receive God's word, then be baptized right away....The Lord's Supper...remember how much God's Son suffered....the core of our worship to God. The body of Christ WAS sinless....How his Son, Jesus, gave his body and his blood to have God's forgiveness....How much wonderful it is!!!! ....Baptism to enter God's family....God loves his only Son and his children....We must preach God's word...even maybe meet ignorance from some people, so we still go on because our purpose is to please God, not God please us.

Professional in Far East in 30s: Jesus was a humble king,who saves the people from sin....Everything is possible which God wants,he can raised the people from death.... A person can recieve God's forgiveness through two ways. When he baptized himself....Change his hearts and lives.

Semi-Professional in Africa in 20s: When we observe our self how God designed to create human being in his Image by calling Holy Spirit,Jesus, God.(Genesis 1:27) ....Our brain used to analyze and think. Genenrally, those who believe in Christ Jesus are one Organ with different function.

Professional in Far East in 40s: Through the teaching of Bible we know that God created human being.... thanks for providing me the very useful informations about the organization of Bible and no doubt it enrich my existing knowledge about Bible..... The story of the suffering servant very much inspired me. He shed his life for the betterment of the other human being. He suffered a lot so that the rest of the human being would be saved from the anger of God. That suffering servant who was predicted came centuries later. He was Jesus who suffered in our place and died in our place on the cross, taking the punishment for our sins on himself .... Through the miracles of Jesus Nicodemus know that Jesus was the son of God.... Jesus was really the Son of God on earth. As a follower of Jesus the lord....

Professional in Middle East in 60s: God as his name (yahweh)... We can be born again spiritually and start life over. We can set free from the power of sin. Jesus did not make empty claims, he demonstrated his divin power with his amazing miracles.... Thank you for all what you did , and what are you doing for some one who connecting to you through God's love.... Faith is, to believe in God as if you can see him, as he sees you. My life a gift from God, and my existential supported by him. Jesus Christ the Son of God, is the Lord and Savior.... They are able to find God as he revealed himself to them through his Son.... Jesus had the power and the heart of God. He had power on earth to forgive the sins, the power of healing the paralysed man. He had power over Satan and the force of evil, and the power bringing the dead back to the life.

Unemployed in Middle East in 30s: Prophet Isaiah when he predicate about Jesus.... the officer knew that he must baptized in a water to start a new life .... Baptism likeness the resurrection, When they immerse their heads they burial , and they became a live new life without sin when their heads up of water .... I am so happy to now all these information about the Christ and Baptize , and I wanna to learn more and more.... We all belive the truth which is the Bibe is the word of God,... I will decide when I will Baptize ..... Now I'm looking for some one who trust in, when I find the person who can baptize me, but I can't send picture, because when I take the picture [of my baptism] for me, it means dead.

Professional in Middle East in 30s: I become aware that the coming king will be a descendant of David and will be called "the Son of God". That is amazing, isn't it?.. I became aware that from beginning to end, the message of the Old Testament is the same: Someone is coming to defeat evil and to save humanity from sin.... she would give a birth to a baby boy who would rule and would defeat satan,... this baby in her was from the Holy Spirit and this son would save people from their sins... I become fully sure now that Jesus was the true king, Jesus was more than a man the miracles did were amazing and proved that he was divine. The word of Jesus is the word of God.... Jesus was really raised from death.... God has already known what would happen to Jesus he made him suffer and went through these painful experiences but God made Jesus free and raised him from death..... Since the officer knew the truth he couldn't stop himself from being baptized.... Jesus is the lord of all people God gives him the Holy Spirit and power to lead people to the right way.... all people will be judged be his Son Jesus Christ.

Student in Far East in 20s: God points ahead to a Savior.... a descendant of Eve will destroy Satan head.... A descendant of Abraham, Isaac, and Jacob will bless all nations..... In these days people still have a hard time understanding what Jesus mean by the new birth.... Jesus was a true king. He can forgive our sin.... gave his life for people

Professional in Far East in 20s: To be a Christian lifelong is difficult .... Jesus is the God with us in form of flesh and clot of blood. He is the supernatural human that ever lived in this mortal universe.... God according to our [Muslim] religious viewpoint has no son and never has a precedent the same to himself but while studying bible I 'm getting some more facts.... he was dying for the sake of truth and humanity.... had to sacrifice even his blood , body and spirit for the sake of truth and love for humanity. Jesus fulfilled the promises of his ancestors.... Yes I agree with you without fail.... God wanted to show his loyalty to the humanity even the fault of His own son. The killers of His son was also forgiven.... Christians Bible is trustworthy and have a lot of evidence to prove its validity.

Semi-Professional in Middle East in 20s: He is greater than any man in the world.... when I follow God and message of Jesus Christ I will be filled with happiness and The Reassuring, I will feel am in safe side....We can not compare him with any king or any person, he is coming from God. I am very impressed in this story, and very sad to Jesus [crucifixion] I wish if I can return the time and be beside him. I Loved him very much. I learned to love Jesus.... Jesus is the truth and no one can deny this truth. .... He is the truth and all that he said about lifting him from death it was truth and not imagination.... When Jesus killed in a cross, God knew this would happen, and realized Jesus must lift from death to be in the right side to him..... The Quran denies this things, really I don't know what I must say. I did not know anything about the Christian religion in the past, but now I know everything. Really I am Happy for that, it is great ..... I feel happy and so excited especially when read the story of Jesus.

Student, in Middle East in 20s: I have learned the importance of new life (to born again) because this part make me feel like, if I born again I may not remember the very bad things that I went through.... He is a spiritual king, and his kingdom is an eternal one that every one of us wishes to be there.... Jesus gave up the ghost so quickly because God didn't want his legs to be broken by the guards.... Change your hearts and lives and be baptized, God will forgive your sins and will give you the gift of the Holy Spirit. This meaningful speech has really touched my heart. ..... it is important because when we baptized we reborn.... I have learned the amazing connection between baptism and Jesus' death, that baptism is a symbol of death, burial and resurrection that's amazing, isn't it?

Professional in Middle East in 30s: Jesus forgave the people who were killing him....Christ's sacrifice and how he gave his own life to take away our sins.

Professional in Middle East in 30s: When the people to be baptized ...will be in the church which is the entrance of kingdom of God on earth....Really God is great to send his son Jesus to defeat Satan.... God wanted his son Jesus to suffer to forgive our sins...God treat us like his childern so he let his son to be killed on a cross to save us, even though he can protect his son but for us that happen.....To believe in God by our heart and to be baptized to share Jesus his raising from death and run away from sins, so we will have the Holy spirit in our bodies and we will be forgiven....Any one from any country who will be follows God and be baptized, will be accepted ....There are many congregations and may have lots of buildings, but there is only one church....Body of Christ is sinless body that was nailed to cross even though that body of Jesus deserved to be a live but he gave his body and his blood to save our life and forgive us even we are sinning bodies....I don't hesitate to admit God loved us through his Son who is Jesus Christ.

Student in Middle East in 20s: At the beginning Mary was scared but then when she felt proud because her son will be Son of God..... Jesus is Son of God.

Professional in Middle East in 40s: The coming [predicted] King will be a descendant of David, his name is "the Son of God" Jesus.

Professional in Far East in 40s: Now I have known that Christians trust in one God, not many. God is a Spirit. ...God can come in human body [Jesus], in tree [to Moses], on paper [in Bible] and where he wants. God came in Jesus and spoke to his creations....Mary was a virgin girl. That baby boy would save humanity from sin.....His name was Jesus (meaning salvation)....The Bible is true holy book of God.....Jesus was the resurrection....Really, Jesus was God's loving........ Jesus has made it possible for every one to have life with him forever. ...This was God plan to humanity to save from sins. ...What a mercy! ...Jesus is ruling over his kingdom. We must change our hearts and lives and be baptized.

Professional in Far East in 30s: God became flesh when Jesus was born. God would send Jesus to save the people from sins....Jesus was the Son of God. He has the Spirit of God...he is eternal.... God saved the human being from sins by sending his Spirit through Jesus.

Professionaal in Far East in 40s: His name was Jesus (meaning salvation)....Jesus declared, the Spirit of God is in me.... The Bible is true holy book of God. ...Jesus was the resurrection. ...Really, Jesus was God's loving.... Jesus has made it possible for every one to have life with him forever. ...This was God plan to humanity to save from sins. ...What a mercy! ...Jesus is ruling over his kingdom. We must change our hearts and lives and be baptized.

Professional in North Africa in early 40s: The Son of God will be a shepherd king....This king will save us from our sins. God's plan was to send his son to relieve us from our sins....Jesus was born to bless us and save us from our bad deeds....A person must be born of water and spirit. Jesus is the true king...the Bible is the Word of God....Different religions confuse people....People of the church...need to be like the angels in heaven [and be messengers] on earth.

Professional in Far East in 40s: Jesus really had been raised from death. ....God will forgive us if we change our hearts and lives and be baptized. Then we also receive the Holy spirit.

Professional in Middle East in 40s: Jesus...gave up is divine nature to become a human....he made Daniel's prediction true....both human and divine. He revealed this by many miracles...to prove his divinity....The meaning behind the Lord's Supper and what it focuses on is truly amazing.

Professional in Middle East in 20s: [After saying many times Jesus was not the Son of 'God....] Jesus Christ is the son of God. He came to change all the world and tell us about the goodness and the awesome God.

Professional in Middle East in 20s: Jesus is... the real Son of God, the only man sent by God to return people from sins. Jesus is still alive and will be alive forever.

Professional in North Africa in 30s: Jesus was not just a man, but God himself and he came to save mankind.

Unknown Occupation in Middle East in 20s: We learned from the Bible...Jesus is the Son of God and all people must believe him....and be baptized in water.

Professional in Middle East in 30s: Peace and Grace Lord Jesus for you. In short, I left Islam because I discovered what follows. (Allah) the God of Islam, in Arabic means "nothing ". Mohammed a liar and insane and not descendants of Ibrahim. The Qur'an is full of lying and myths and incitement to murder and hatred. Many parts of the Koran written by followers of

Mohammed for political purposes after his death. Islam cancels the role of reason Islam is the reason for the backwardness and ignorance. If there is a beautiful thing in Islam it is taken from Christianity I am responsible for what I say. I have worked hard in reading to obtain such information's. I Have a lot to say about Christianity, But I will mention one thing. When I heard a sermon mountain I cried and I cried and I cried and then decided that this speech must be the Lord....When I knew Jesus, I felt great happiness [but] people hit me....I believe Jesus was and is the God who created everything.

Professional in Middle East in 20s: After we receive the Spirit of God, we will be look like Jesus"....We must think about Jesus sacrificing for us....Jesus is the only Son of God and Christians are considered the children of God. The Spirit of God will live in us after baptism.

Profesional in Middle East in 30s: He was not a regular person....Christ was both A human and a heavenly person. The Word and the Son of God refer to Jesus Christ.... He sacrificed himself to save the believers who sinned from ctcrnal death.... he was sacrificed for the sins of mankind.

Professsional in North Africa in 30s: Jesus,God's word and spirit given to virgin Mary....Jesus claimed to be the eternal, self-existent one."...unification of the Godhead....he was calling God his own father making himself equal with God....He was Immanuel , meaning God with us..... No one from the very early begging of the life till now can do what Jesus did....we grow into the likeness of Christ--who is exactly like God.

Professional in Central Africa in early 20s: The new king who will be ruling over God's kingdom. The king will be different from other kings, will be inspired by the Spirit of God and will speak for God....it was foretold hundreds years ago that descendant of David would be the king of jews and the Son of God.....He is really God's Son....I really learned that Jesus is the

Son of God for sure. He has been sent from heaven no be served but to serve .

Professional in Middle East in 40s: The church will represent the kingdom of God if the people which is made up of, calling Out their sins, living like angles.... Should be complete that by baptizing himself in water.... which proved that the Jesus of the Bible New Testament is fact, Jesus and his true bible will stay represent the glory and majesty and he deserves all respect from all people on the earth.... no contradiction between the divinity of Jesus and the Old Testament Doctrine of monotheism

Professional in North Africa in 40s: A descendant of David and will be called "the Son of God".... he existed before Abraham was born.....His words are the words of God.... God will forgive our sins if we Change our hearts and lives and be baptized, in the name of Jesus Christ.

Semi-Professional in North Africa in 20s: Jesus is the king who will save the humanity.... her son would be The Son of God....your words were all I need. Now I understand it, and I belive in it....Jesus is the true king....It is a war, which I intend to win it by following the savior Jesus.... a man can be born again with a new pure spirit to follow Jesus teachings....He is God's son and the Word that all things were made through....when Jesus forgave those who were torturing him. I will not forget this!

Professional in Far East in 40s: Mary was blessed by a son called Jesus who is called "the Son of Lord God". She became the virgin mother of God's Son, Jesus....Jesus was the Son of God....He was the Son of God and God anointed him. He held the power to do anything in the world because he was the Son of God.

Professional in Middle East in 20s: Jesus is the king of people and angels. Jesus kingdoms were includes haven and earth..... Now, I start reading the Bible, even in different language

Christianity or Islam ~ The Contrast

and I saw that is a great book and help me to understand more about the reason behind our existing as human being... I really want to know more about the Christianity.... I felt always afraid from hell and I search to satisfy God in my behave and action.... I have learned a lot of information and I called knowledge of our soul. It is not that easy to be a christian in my culture. I don't know if you hide your passionate toward a religion will be a sin. . I am waiting for the right moment when I can found the peace inside me. Life here make me confuse in a lot of things. I am really not comfortable with my life at all here because of the bad situation. Many people were dead every day, especially in my city.

Professional in Middle East in 20s: Mary became mother of the lord, mother of the king....he is the son of God, he is the God's words....tell me more about being baptized.

Semi-Professional in Far East in 20s: RIYAZ Jesus was crucified and raised from death.... A person receives God's forgiveness today by baptizing himself, by turning away from sin and by following the good things.... Jesus revealed his divine identity by his words and deeds.... Jesus was also a divine.

Professional in Far East in 20s: Every person who believes in God and Jesus will be forgiven.... in the oneness of God....there is only one God and Jesus was His son, he was crucified on our sins, he would come back one day and judge all the people, and his followers will be entered in his kingdom.

Semi-Professional in Europe in 30s: He is son of God and he was killed by the people. He saved humanity from sin by giving away his life.

Professional in Middle East in early 50s: Baptism is a great chance to live a new life without sins.... he shoud be baptized to be a true christian.... Bible and Jesus are true.... Jesus was and still a great divine figure....Jesus a divine and an earthly creature at the same time...., he was supernatural and lived as any human lived, but without sin....He sacrificed his life to make us live spiritually and physically....Bible itself proved that they were the word of God....death of oour sins, a new life for us.

Semi-Professional in Middle East in 30s: Jesus did a lot of miracles by using God name and proved his divine.... be baptized in water and make clean himself from sin..... Baptism can give them new life and heart and its mean that after baptism, everyone will be clean from .... Jesus claimed to be the eternal, self-existent one.... Jesus was both human and divine .... The Bible is the Word of God.... the words of Jesus are the words of God.

Semi-Professional in North Africa in 40s: The Bible guide to humanity to become the kind believers of one God.... People worship him as Son of God. Jesus is really a son of God as most people believe in that.... Jesus proved that he was the son of God.

Semi-Professional in North Africa in 20s: Jesus sacrificed himself....returned to life after his death.... forgives all the people who changed their heart, their lives and baptize.... Jesus and his followers under attack, because the natural of human, rejects all new . Also people don't know the truth of Jesus and his flowers.

Semi-Professional in Middle East in 30s: He had a power and holy spirit from the lord; this prove that he is son of God.... he is the lord.... God's word rise and defeat the evil....Jesus was God's soul....The lord commanded people, if they believed in him to baptize.

Retiree in Middle East in 50s: He was son of God, the true King and can free people from sin....God send to people his son....He domonstrated his divine power....How is it possible to become a Christian?

Semi-Professional in North Africa in mid-20s: Interested in

christian religion ...I have learnt an interested biblical story.... prediction for coming of Jesus.... this painful topic on how Jesus was arrested...and finally killed....God's beloved son.... God's forgiveness: To repent for the wrong which you have been doing, To be baptised, and finally change of our hearts and lives.

Blue Collar worker in United States in 40s: ...believed that is truly a divine person.... Jesus is the king of kings he is the son of God.

Semi-Professional in Middle East in 40s: ...killed his son on a cross.... Jesus Said (I am). "I am the Alpha and the Omega . . who is, and who was, and who is to come, the Almighty."....I can be a daughter of God who see and reflect his glory.

University student in Middle East in 20s: The Christ the Son of God not natural but by God's spirit.... Jesus promised the Christians will be with them always. even the end of world....We must hange our hearts, lives and be baptized.

Semi-Professional in Middle East in 30s: He is a holy prophet came from heaven this prove that he is son of God. .... he is the lord and he has a holy spirit from God....The lord commanded people, if they believed in him to baptize.... he is divine, his power and strength from his lord. He comes to prove that he has the magic word. "The voice of GOD". ... he is divine and his spiritual soul comes from the glory God. ... He sacrifice and gives us the life, took the sins away, his blood saves us today

Professional in Middle East in 20s: Jesus is closer to angels than people....I want to read more from the Bible.... Jesus was an ideal man because he has special characteristics like sinless.... Jesus and God is the same...." your sins are forgiven", this indicate his divine identity.

Professional in Middle East in 30s: I have discovered that the king coming will be David descendants who called son of God he will be a shepherd king.... Jesus is the Christ , the Messiah and true king. The words of God is the Bible. It is never too late to start life again make a fresh started . All our past mistakes and failures be buried and forgotten when any one baptism .

University Student in Africa, in 20s: .... building my faith and making me strong in the Lord.... no matter how deep you are into sins God can and will wash you to be whole again.... the inspirirng chapters of the Bible.... Jesus is life, the way, the light, the world, and The Son of God.... Jesus is really the son of God and that no matter our circumstance we should always give thanks to God.... changing our heart and our lives, and also been baptizinno.

Professional in Middle East in 20s: People are baptised in the name of Jesus to recive God's forgivness.

University of Student in Eurasia in 20s: This prophet will be the son of God will come to save the sinners..... He had a divine character and directed by the Holy Spirit. and did not anything that is of will of men.

Student in North Africa in late teens: Jesus was the one who sacrificed his life to save others from sin.... I really respect and appreciate what you do Mum because challenging a religon is not easy at all to know which God is the right one and gladly you achieved....Jesus "Son of God" had great powers and...proved he is eternal.

Christianity or Islam ~ The Contrast

Professional in North Africa in 30s: one needs to be born again in order to become a full flesh member of God kingdom. I have learned about important of being baptize, for it wash away one sin and gives an opportunity of starting a new life. I have learned that Jesus died for our sake, to cleanse our sin and gives us the opportunity to be a true member of God kingdom.... baptize in the name of the father, the son and the holy spirit.

Epidemiologist near Russia in early 40s: he was son of God. Jesus was the one who love all people although the people who want kill him.

Instituter in North Africa in early 40s: Jesus belong to God as his Father, and God called Jesus "My Son." Jesus proved that He was the Man who would crash the Satan's head.

Teacher in Middle East, in 20s: Jesus had a father-son relationship with God. The Son of God send to earth to seprate people from sins.

Student in Middle East in teens: I think Christian is the right way. Christianity is the righteous religion in the world, it is God kingdom, all human being. Baptism symbolize, we are burred with our lord Jesus, and also we died with him. Baptism lead us to a new life and eternal life. I have learned our old sin will be washed when we are Baptized.

Tour director in near Russia in late 30s: He was the Son of God in spiritual way. The way he was born shows us that he was sent by God. What he said and what he did was all done by the will of God. Believing in Jesus means believing in God.

Unemployed in Europe in early 30s: when a person is baptised his sins are forgiven and we learn to love each other and become holy and pure. Our hearts become free from guiltless when we are washed from the blood of Christ and pure water.

Teacher in S. Europe in mid-40s: Jesus was the Son of God sent into the world to save it through him.

Student in Middle East in late 30s: Isaiah and other prophets predicted a prophet i.e. Jesus, Son of God will come to earth. He will be a common man who will be punished and suffer for the sins of humanity. He will born to a virgin women. He will die but will come back to life and will live for forever.

Biologist in Africa in early 30s: Jesus is the only true son of the living God sent in order to show us the right way that leads to God. Jesus is really the saviour of the world. I think the Bible is the best book ever written. He was sent to wash our sins.

Researcher in Middle East in early 50s: Jesus is the son of God, it's not meaning that he is a son as same us that we have parents so God is his father same as our father, but because he called for himself 'SON OF GOD' and 'LORD MY FATHER' and others also called for him 'SON OF GOD', it's mean that he has spirit of God and God is in.

Biologist in Africa in early 50s: In spiritual way Jesus is the son of God . The relationship between God and Jesus is like a father and his wife . They love each other very much. He is the son of God. So God gave him the power over all things.

A FORMER MUSLIM'S STORY

I was born in a family that belonged to the Sunni Muslim sect. The area I was raised in was the Shi-ite Muslim sect.
So I was able to be exposed to the whole Muslim community ~ secular, Sunni and Shi'ite.
I tried to be an especially good Muslim. Sometimes I

followed the Sunnis. But when I became dissatisfied with them, I flipped to the Shi-ites. Eventually I discarded both. I just couldn't communicate with my Allah and approach him because he was so scary:

A god commanding that hands or arms be cut off as punishment, or beheading.

A god who commands racism and oppression or killing of anyone who opposes him.

A god who shows favoritism to men and deprives the women of rights.

A god who changed his words [Qu'ran] many times.

A god who asks you to send your son to blow himself up, taking innocent lives with him for his pleasure.

I couldn't find a replacement, so I gave up since there were not enough resources or freedom to study or search. But

my personality from inside was deeply wounded because I was missing something. I always felt a "Mysterious Power" was taking care of me. So I started to ask that Power to reveal himself to me. I was playing with fire because I was questioning everything in my culture.

Then I got my first study BIBLE. It was in both Arabic and English.

The thing that caught my attention is what was underlined ~ John 8:32 ("Then you will know the truth and the truth will set you free"). That was just a new challenge. But I kept wondering what is the truth. Is it historical fact, or scientific fact, or something else? I knew there was no absolute truth.

Still I wanted to know the truth to be free because that was my first concern,. Later I found another interesting thing about the truth in the same gospel ~John 14:6 ("Jesus answered, 'I am the way and the truth and the life. No one comes to the father except through me.' ") That was an amazing theory.

Then I started to pray to the Christian God to reveal himself to me and show me the right teaching I was looking for ~ the teaching based on love, peace, freedom. The teaching that makes you proud to be a human being, to be treated with respect and dignity.

Then I discovered another verse in Jeremiah 29:11 (" For I know the plans I have for you,' declares the Lord. 'Plans to prosper you, not to harm you. Plans to give you hope and a future.' ")

I went to the Church and I asked...to baptize me...by immersion. I was happy because in my opinion this time I knew what I did was based on God's rules. Basically the church I attend shared with me more or less the same doctrine like baptism by immersion, confession, faith, repentance, unity, keeping the Lord's Supper, contributing, and the Bible as the only guide. Thank you, Jesus, for your blood that freed me from my sin and reconciled me again with God the father.

48. Open Letter to Our Muslim Friends

(Long, but sincere)

Dear friend.

This is a personal letter from the author to you.

The first time I read the Qur'an, it was hard for me. I had grown up in a part of the world where people use the Scriptures (Tanakh) of the Book as Yahweh (the I AM)'s holy word, and consider the writings of all other religions wrong. It was hard for me to read about Allah creating the world, and the prophet Abraham (Ibrahim) obeying Allah.

So I can imagine how hard it may have been for you to read the Book (Bible). It must have been hard for you to read about Yahweh (the I AM) creating the world, and the prophet Abraham (peace be upon him) obeying Yahweh (the I AM).

You are in good company. Many Muslims (also Hindus, Buddhists, atheists, etc.) have gone through the same thing you have ~ reading a holy book that they were raised to believe was corrupted.

I understand the deep commitment that Muslims have for only One God. And for the prophet Mohammed being the last prophet. And the Qur'an being written in order to bring new revelations.

I understand praying five times a day (salat) and giving to the poor (zakat) and fasting (sawm). I have fasted for as long as three days and nights at a time. I give a percent of my income every Sunday and periodically take food and clothing to be given to the poor. I pray many times a day. The Book says to pray without ceasing; so I am never very far from prayer throughout the day. (By the way, I hope you remember each day when you wake up that I prayed for you that same day.)

I also understand that you and I are in a fight with Satan

over our souls. We do not want to go to hell. There is a lot at stake here ~ our eternity that never ends. It's frightening! What if you and I have been worshiping the wrong God all these years? It's kind of like being half way across a bridge over a gully hundreds of feet deep and suddenly finding out the bridge is about to collapse! We thought we were safe, but we thought wrong! It was the wrong path. Such a thought is terrifying!

If you and I had been born in India, we undoubtedly would have been raised to be good Hindus. If we had been born in Malaysia, we undoubtedly would have been raised to be good Buddhists. If we had been born in Communist China or Communist Russia, we undoubtedly would have been raised to be good atheists. So much of what we are and believe today is a result of where we happened to have been born ~ accident of birth.

Several years ago I decided to challenge the religion my parents had taught me. Was Christianity true and the Yahweh (the I AM) of the Christians the right God? So I read from the Hindu holy writings, the Buddhist holy writings, and even the writings of atheists. Of course, I also read the Qur'an, as I said earlier. So, with all of them claiming to be the only religion, how could I decide which one was true?

I looked for built-in proofs. I looked in vain. Finally, I found many scientific facts in the Book that were not known when written by the prophets. Proofs scattered throughout the Book were predictions of the fall of entire kingdoms often centuries after the prophet died. The prophet could not have known the future on his own. Since those predictions were true, the rest of that Book must be true. Do you remember when I sent you the list of those Bible predictions which were verified by the Encyclopedia Britannica? If I hadn't found those proofs, I would have never believed the Book was the unchangeable Truth.

But what about the "trinity" you have heard that Christians claim while at the same time claiming there is only one God, *and the Holy Spirit; and these three are one* [Injil, I John 5:7]. ? The term "trinity" is not in the Book. However, I did find this: *For there are three that bear witness in heaven: the Father, the Word*

So, what is so different about you and I being committed to two different religions? This takes us back to what I said earlier ~ our deep fear of hell. I think one main difference between us is HOW to be saved from hell.

The Qur'an says there is one angel on our left (shoulder?) and one on our right (shoulder?) writing down everything we do right and everything we do wrong [Surah 46:19]. Since sometimes we sin when we do not realize we are sinning, how are we to know if we're saved? Must we wait until the Day of Judgment when the scales are brought out and it's too late to change anything [Surah 10:6-10]?

Further, the Qur'an says God forgives our sins, but he remembers them all over again on the Day of Judgment as though they had never been forgiven. But the God of the Bible says, "I will forgive them, and remember their sins no more."

My dear, dear friend. We do not have to fear death and the Judgment. You and I can know right now if we're saved from hell! Isn't that what you want? You and I want to know we have defeated Satan and will be saved from hell to live forever with God. Isn't that why you and I pray and fast and give alms and love God so much?

Remember Adam and Eve (peace be upon them)? Remember how sin separated them from God? Why? Because God is Perfect and absolute Goodness. It is just as impossible for God to dwell with sin as it is for God to sin! This means that, even if we did more good deeds than bad in our lifetime, we would still be sinners. It only takes one sin to be a sinner. So, how to solve this Great Dilemma? Eternal justice demands that sin must be punished before it can be erased.

Injil John 1:1&14 in the Book says, "*In the beginning was the Word, and the Word was with God, and the Word was God....The Word became flesh and made his dwelling among us. We have seen his glory, the glory of the One and Only (God).*" How can God, the Word, be the One and Only and be in a human body too? It's like when you put your words into a tape recorder. There aren't suddenly two of you. You have simply put your words in the tape recorder. God spoke to Moses (peace be upon him) in a burning tree [Surah

28:30]. Does that mean God was now two ~ one God in heaven and one God in the burning tree? No. In the same way, Yahweh (the I AM) put his words in a human body but remained One God.

Well, why was the Word of Yahweh (the I AM) on earth also called the Son of Yahweh (the I AM) since he was not conceived like humans? He had many titles. In a prophecy about him [Tanakh Sahaif Isaiah 9:6], he was called a Son, Wonderful Counselor, Mighty God, Everlasting Father, Prince of Peace. (Of course, that didn't make him five Gods; he is still one.)

Perhaps the Word was also sometimes called the Son in order to help us understand the kind of relationship we can have with the Creator of the World. Injil Romans 6: 3-4 in the Book says when you and I go through the ritual cleansing of baptism, our old sinful nature dies and is buried and we are reborn through God the Father. Then we become God's child, not his slave. Injil Ephesians 1:4-5 in the Book says, *"For he chose us in him before the creation of the world to be holy and blameless in his sight in love; he predestined us to be adopted as his sons through Jesus Christ, in accordance with his pleasure and will."*

But why would Yahweh (the I AM) put His voice in a human body? Because that human body's voice carried to us Yahweh's (the I AM's) voice that we could hear. Also, because that human body was needed for mankind to see Someone who was perfect. And finally, so that human body could take our place and take the punishment for our sins.

Do you recall a time in your life when someone said they did some bad thing that you actually did? Perhaps an older brother or sister did this for you. Why? So they could take your punishment for you, being stronger than you. This is exactly what that human body whom we call Jesus (Issa) did for us. He was stronger than us.

Remember Adam and Eve (peace be upon them) sinning in the Garden of Eden? Sin causes us to be separated from God. It is called spiritual death. On the cross, Jesus (Issa) cried out that Yahweh (the I AM) had forsaken him. He went through that spiritual death in your place and in my place! Why did he do it?

Because only He could make his way back to Yahweh (the I AM) ~ something impossible for us to do. I think that perhaps He also went to hell during those dark hours on the cross. Why? Because only He could break out of hell ~ something else impossible for us to do.

Finally, that human body died physically and was buried for three days. Then, that human body came back to life ~ a third thing impossible for us to do. That human body ~ Jesus ~ overcame both spiritual death and physical death for us!

Then Yahweh (the I AM) announced to the world that he would forgive anyone who believed these things happened, and who was willing to die, be buried and come back to life. How is that possible? By dying to our sinful nature ~ the part of us that sins and doesn't care ~ then being buried in water, then coming up out of the water a new-born soul. We can KNOW WE ARE SAVED FROM HELL! We don't have to spend the rest of our life worrying and wondering if we were good enough, and dreading the Day of Judgment. Our faith and burial in water not only makes us good enough, but it makes us perfect in Yahweh's (the I AM's) eyes!

> *Come to me, all you who are weary and burdened,*
> *And I will give you rest.*
> *Take my yoke upon you and learn from me,*
> *For I am gentle and humble in heart,*
> *And you will find rest for your souls.*
>
> *Jesus the Messiah*
> *[Injil Matthew 11:28]*

My dear, dear friend. You and I both want to be saved from hell. You and I both want to live forever in heaven with God. I am entreating you. Please go through the cleansing ritual of baptism.

Yes, I know that most if not all of your friends are Muslims and your family is. First, Yahweh (the I Am) knows their hearts and whether they would have become Christians if they had been able to read the Book. Perhaps some of your Muslim friends and family tried to talk you out of reading from the Book. You resisted them. You have shown great strength. I AM SO PROUD OF YOU! Now is time to take it to the next level up.

Dare to be baptized in the name of (by the authority of) the Father, the Spirit and the Word. Yahweh (the I AM) is gracious, merciful and forgiving. Praise be to Yahweh (the I AM) for ever and ever!

Will it take courage? Of course it will! But Yahweh (the I AM) will be with you to give you strength. The Apostle Paul (peace be upon him) was put in prison for believing this and wrote, "*It has become clear throughout the whole palace guard and to everyone else that I am in chains for Christ. Because of my chains, most of the brothers in the Lord have been encouraged to speak the word of God more courageously and fearlessly*" [Injil Philippians 1:13-14].

Remember the prophet Abraham (peace be upon him) and how Yahweh (the I AM) called him out of the religion of his family and neighbors? Was it easy for him to do? Of course not! But he was courageous and went against them and believed Yahweh's (the I AM's) promises to protect him. Yahweh (the I AM) promises you, *"Never will I leave you; never will I forsake you"* and *"The Lord is my helper, I will not be afraid"* [Injil Hebrews 13:5-6]. Praise be to Yahweh (the I AM) who will be your strength!

Have you ever tried praying to Yahweh (the I AM)? Would you try it right now? It will be strange to you. But He will hear you. No, it's not reciting the Book; it is words from your heart to Yahweh's (the I AM's) heart. Go ahead! Right now!

Please listen to what I'm trying to tell you! Never again will you have to believe that the only sure way to go to heaven is to be a martyr [Surahs 22, 47, etc.]! Never again will you have to believe that you must fight for Allah [Surahs 2, 4, 8, 9, 47, 48, 61, etc.] Never again will you have to believe that all your bad and good deeds are being weighed against each other to see if you will go to heaven or hell [Surahs 2, 4, 21, 22, 29, 30, 45, 46, 50, 57, 99, 101, etc.].

I'm talking about your eternal soul! What if you died next week? You don't think it's possible? There are some 7 billion people in the world. Every hour some 665 people die. By the time you get up in the morning, clean up and get dressed, then have a little breakfast, 665 souls have died and met Judgment. One of them could be you in the next hour or day. People die from accidents, diseases, disasters. The husband of a friend of mine, just 29 years old, died in an accident at work a few weeks ago. No one knows when their time on earth will be up. No one knows when there will be no more chances. Injil Hebrews 9:27 says, "Man is destined to die once, and after that to face judgment."

Do you know the final and eternal destination of your soul? You CAN know! Just follow the FIVE PILLARS of Salvation: (1) Read the scriptures (Tanakh). (2) Believe the scriptures (Tanakh) that Jesus (Issa) was God's Word on earth in a human body that died in your place. (3) Repent of your sins. (4) Confess that you believe Jesus (Issa) was God's Word on earth. (5) Be baptized to bury your sinful nature and be reborn into the Royal Family of God. (6) Lead a faithful Christian life. Will you be baptized too?

My dear, dear friend. The Qur'an teaches that only martyrs are <u>guaranteed</u> salvation [Surah 22:58]. Everyone else has to wait until Judgment Day to see if they did more good deeds than bad deeds. In baptism you can be a spiritual martyr! Aren't you dying to your sinful nature? Aren't you being buried in water to bury your sins? Aren't you then guaranteed salvation? The only difference is that you come back to life!

The cleansing ritual of baptism is honorable but simple. If you live in a country where you will be arrested, imprisoned and killed for becoming a Christian, ask a relative or close friend willing to baptize you in secret. If you are not near any trustworthy relatives or friends and do not have money to go to where someone will baptize you safely, it is better to be baptized any way you can than remain unbaptized for years and taking the chance of dying in that state.

You just say (or whisper) "I believe Jesus is the Son/Word of God." Next, you say (or whisper) that you are being baptized in the name (authority) of God the Father, the Word, and the Spirit. Then, just as Jesus died bearing your sins, you die to your sinful nature, the part of you that sins and doesn't care. Next, just as Jesus was buried in his grave, you lower yourself all the way under your watery "grave". Then, just as Jesus rose up out of his grave the Savior, you rise up out of your watery grave the Saved!

Be brave! You can do it! It only takes minutes, but it will affect your eternity. After your baptism, you will have the strength of God in your heart, the Word of God in your mind, and God's Holy Spirit in your soul. Praise be to our almighty Yahweh (the I AM) who calls himself LOVE!

What will your life be like as a Christian? It will be wonderful! You will have an inner peace you never thought possible. You may have to be baptized in secret and worship in secret. On the first day of every week, you read some from the Bible if you can, and pray. You also keep the holy Communion (Lord's Supper) by taking a bite of unleavened bread which represents Jesus' body hung on the cross for you, and prayerfully thanking God for this; then by taking a sip of grape juice which represents Jesus' blood shed on the cross for you, and prayerfully thanking God for this. I will send you a simple Sunday worship guide each week that you can do in your own native language alone or with family in secret. It will have a different spiritual theme each week.

Early Christians faced persecution on all sides by both Jews and idol worshipers. Injil II Corinthians says of some early Christians, "*As servants of God we commend ourselves in every way: In great endurance, in troubles, hardships and distresses; in beatings, imprisonments and riots; in hard work, sleepless night and hunger....I have been in prison more frequently, been flogged more severely and been exposed to death again and again. Five times I received from the Jews the forty lashes minus one. Three times I was beaten with rods, once I was stoned.*"

But these early Christians stubbornly believed and never, never, never renounced their faith. At the end of his life, the Apostle Paul said in Injil II Timothy, "*I am suffering even to the point of being chained like a criminal. But God's word is not chained....If we died with him (Jesus), we will also live with him; if we endure, we will also reign with him.... I am already being poured out like a drink offering, and the time has come for my departure (death). I have fought the good fight. I have finished the race. I have kept the faith. Now there is in store for me the crown of righteousness which the Lord, the righteous Judge, will award to me on that day ~ and not only to me, but also to all who have longed for his appearing."*

I am not saying these things will happen to you. But can you be brave like that? I know you can. It will all be worth it. Heaven is for eternity. Suffering here is for but a little while. Nothing is hidden from Yahweh (the I AM); He is all seeing, all knowing, and all merciful. He sees you. He knows you by name. Yahweh (the I AM) is all powerful, and will personally give you a share of His power.

Another former Muslim, now a Christian, said about his baptism, *"I arranged it very secretly, otherwise I will be ruined by jail at least. I don't deny that I was not relaxed while I was being baptized because of the conditions and dark atmosphere, and my family was extremely worried, but everything is okay now. Now I want to serve what I love ~ Christianity."*

> *In all these things we are more than conquerors*
> *through him who loved us.*
> *For I am convinced that neither death nor life,*
> *Neither angels nor demons,*
> *Neither the present nor the future,*
> *Nor any powers,*
> *Neither height nor depth,*
> *Nor anything else in all creation*
> *Will be able to separate us from*
> *The love of God that is in Christ Jesus our Lord.*
>
> [Injil, Romans 8:37-39]

You are so very special to me. I am so worried about your soul and where you will spend eternity. Jesus Christ (Issa Al-Masih) is our only hope. What are you waiting for?

My heart touches your heart. I am your soul friend, and, if you become a Christian, I will remain your friend through everything you go through the rest of your life until the day I die.

I will give you moral and spiritual support. This is a promise! You will never be alone. I cannot save you from persecution, but I will always be your friend. Yahweh (the I AM) will give you his Holy Spirit who will give you strength you never thought possible and you will thrive through Jesus (Issa) the Word. Finally, in heaven we will be together, not in self-indulgence as the Quran says, but in worshiping at the very throne of Yahweh ~ the GREAT I AM!

Yours in the service of Al Hazrat Issa, Al Masih, Al Kalimat Allah,

Mum Katheryn

Helpful Links
For Further Study

Free Injil (New Testament) of the Bible in Arabic:
(Not mailed to the Middle East for your safety.)
https://casagrandechurchofchrist.com/free-arabic-bible/

Download the Bible in Your Native Language and English
(We suggest you put it on a flash drive and
bury it in your yard.)
http://www.bibleleague.org/resources/bible-download

Read Bible in two languages side by side
https://wordproject.org/bibles/parallel/b/arabic.htm

Searchable Quran in Several Translations
http://www.searchtruth.com/list.php

Movie About the Life of Christ in Many Languages
http://www.inspirationalfilms.com

Topics in this book on a website in Arabic
https://casagrandechurchofchrist.com/islam-christianity/

Learn English Using the Bible As a Text Book
(secure website)
https://www.worldenglishinstitute.org/register

Beginner's Lessons on the Bible
(secure website)
http://www.worldbibleschool.org

Buy Your Next Book Now

CHRISTIAN LIFE
Applied Christianity: Handbook 500 Good Works
You Can Be a Hero Alone
Worship Changes Since 1st Century + Worship 1sr Century Way
The Best of Alexander Campbell's Millennial Harbinger
Inside the Hearts of Bible Women-Reader+Audio+Leader
The Lord's Supper: 52 Readings with Prayers
http://bit.ly/Christianlife

BIBLE TEXT STUDIES
Revelation: A Love Letter From God
The Holy Spirit: 592 Verses Examined
Was Jesus God? (Why Evil)
365 Life-Changing Scriptures Day by Date
Love Letters of Jesus & His Bride, Ecclesia
Christianity or Islam? The Contrast
The Road to Heaven
http://bit.ly/BibleTexts

FUN BOOKS
Bible Puzzles, Bible Song Book, Bible Numbers
http://bit.ly/BibleFun

TOUCHING GOD SERIES
365 Golden Bible Thoughts: God's Heart to Yours
365 Pearls of Wisdom: God's Soul to Yours
365 Silver-Winged Prayers: Your Spirit to God's
http://bit.ly/TouchingGodSeries

-SURVEY SERIES: EASY BIBLE WORKBOOKS
→Old Testament & New Testament Surveys
→Questions You Have Asked-Part I & II
http://bit.ly/BibleWorkbooks

HISTORICAL RESEARCH BIBLE
for Novel, Screenwriter, Documentary & Thesis Writers
http://bit.ly/32uZkHa

GENEALOGY: How to Climb Your Family Tree Without Falling Out
Volume I & 2: Beginner-Intermediate & Colonial-Medieval
http://bit.ly/GenealogyBeginner-Advanced

About the Author

Katheryn Maddox Haddad grew up in Dearborn, Michigan and attended school with many Muslims with whom she was friends. She now lives in Arizona where she does not have to shovel sunshine. She basks in 100-degree weather with palm trees, cacti, and a computer with most of the lettering worn off.

She has a bachelor's degree in English, Bible, and history, from Harding University, a Master's Degree in management and human relations from Abilene Christian University, and part of a Master's Degree in Bible from the Harding School of Theology.

She spends half her day writing, and the other half teaching English over the internet worldwide using the Bible as text book. Students she has converted to Christianity are in hiding in Afghanistan, Iran, Iraq, Uzbekistan, Tajikistan, Yemen, Somalia, Jordan Sierra Leone, Indonesia, Algeria, and Palestine. To date, she has taught some 7,000 Muslims and has had a long-term friendship with many of them.

In addition to her books, she has written numerous articles for *Gospel Advocate, Twenty-First Century Christian, Firm Foundation, Christian Bible Teacher, Christian Woman,* and several other publications. Her weekly column, *Little-Known Facts About the Bible,* appeared several years in newspapers in North Carolina and Texas.

Connect with Katheryn Maddox Haddad

Website: https://inspirationsbykatheryn.com

Facebook: bit.ly/FacebooksKatherynMaddoxHaddad

Linkedin: http://bit.ly/KatherynLinkedin

Twitter: https://twitter.com/KatherynHaddad

Pinterest: https://www.pinterest.com/haddad1940/

Goodreads:
https://www.goodreads.com/katherynmaddoxhaddad

Get A Free Book

Sign up for Katheryn's monthly newsletter with half-price books for the whole family and insider tips on what's coming next. http://bit.ly/katheryn

If you liked this book kindly place a review on
Your favorite bookseller's website
SO OTHERS WILL BE ENCOUAGED TO READ IT
AND BE INSPIRED.

www.ingramcontent.com/pod-product-compliance
Lightning Source LLC
Chambersburg PA
CBHW071619080526
44588CB00010B/1189